Social Style/
Management Style

Social Style/ Management Style

Developing Productive Work Relationships

Robert Bolton
Dorothy Grover Bolton

amacom

American Management Associations

This book is available at a special
discount when ordered in bulk quantities.
For information, contact Special Sales Department,
American Management Associations, Publications Group,
135 West 50th Street, New York, NY 10020.

Library of Congress Cataloging in Publication Data

Bolton, Robert.
    Social style/management style.

    Includes bibliographical references and index.
    1. Psychology, Industrial.   I. Bolton, Dorothy
Grover.   II. Title.
    HF5548.8.B635   1984   158′.26   83-45959
    ISBN 0-8144-5703-7
    ISBN 0-8144-7617-1 (pbk.)

Printing number

10 9 8 7 6 5 4 3 2 1

To
Dorie and Rose
—our mothers, who have chosen the course of courage, love,
and faith, and whose consistent support has been present even
in times when it has been most difficult to give.

Preface

Whether you are a top executive, a middle manager, a first-line supervisor, an accountant, or a secretary, your success depends largely on your ability to deal with other human beings. A manager is, by definition, a specialist in relating to people. His prime job is to get results with and through other people. In varying degrees this is true of virtually every type of position in the modern workplace. People who are not in managerial roles often find themselves increasingly involved with people. This book is designed to help you become more effective in the critically important interpersonal dimension of your work.

The ability to understand and relate to different working styles is one of the most useful ways of forging effective work relationships. Recently, many approaches to understanding working styles have been developed. Of all the models, we find the social style concept by far the most practical for the workplace. Easy to learn and relatively easy to apply, it tends to be nonthreatening and has a sound basis in theory, research, and experience.

By far the most significant and practical contribution to our understanding of the social style concept came from the work of the industrial psychologists David Merrill, Ph.D., and Roger Reid, M.A. Their computer-assisted research on social style began in the early 1960s and is still continuing. Their research team helped us and many other consultants learn about the fundamentals of social style. Our indebtedness to Merrill's and Reid's identification of the two basic dimensions of social styles, their description of the four styles, and many of their concepts of how to use style effectively is clear to those who read their *Personal Styles and Effective Performance: Make Your Style Work For You*.[1] In some instances our definitions of terms and our point of view differ from Merrill's and Reid's. Some readers will want to examine the Merrill–Reid volume to see both the similarities and the differences in the two works.

Our understanding of social style has been enriched by the findings of practitioners and theorists whose collective work spans 24 centuries of history beginning with Hippocrates (c460–c370 BC), the founder of modern medicine, and extending through Carl Jung, one of the towering figures of modern psychology.[2] The extensive leadership studies conducted under Carroll Shartle's direction at Ohio State University in the late 1940s and early 1950s had a significant impact on our thinking about management styles.[3] Fred Fiedler's writings helped liberate us from the idea that there is one "best" managerial style for all occasions.[4] And William Reddin's managerial effectiveness model clarified important areas for us.[5]

To gain a better understanding of people types, we've read in fields as varied as psychology, anthropology, management, education, sales, history, medicine, and philosophy. Even the least helpful books usually provided some insight.[6–46] Sometimes we probed fairly deeply into topics that, in our minds, were related to social style (self-esteem, for example). Finally, we read hundreds of biographies to see how social style was illustrated in the lives of famous people. Conducting interviews and reviewing audio- and videotapes were also part of our research methodology.

Richard Strauss said, "Ideas, like young wine, should be put in storage and taken up again only after they have been allowed to ferment and to ripen."[47] That pretty well describes the process we used in developing this book. We pondered our experience, read extensively, and thought some more. Then we wrote and revised several previous editions of this volume—reading, experimenting, and mulling between each edition.

Why another book on social style? A topic so important to improved performance and enriched relationships requires continuous development. We think we have made important additions to social style theory here. Some of the applications of the model to the workplace go beyond what is available in the literature to date (although our commitment to writing a short book means that many of these applications will be developed in a future volume). Finally, we have received feedback that the brevity of the book and its format make it useful for busy people who are looking for practical ways to improve their performance.

Many of the ideas in this book will come not as news but as reminders. This volume contains much material that everybody knows. Yet we are told that this way of organizing interpersonal data helps people use what they have already learned from life experience. Readers of earlier editions have told us that, because the ideas are so closely related to what they already understand, the new learnings are easier to implement.

Most participants in our courses express a preference for a concise presentation of information in books, workbooks, and handouts. We've tried to be flexible about our style to respond to that preference. Four appendixes provide further information for those who wish it. Also, we have provided considerable detail in the notes and references at the end of the book so that those interested can further explore working styles and social style theory and practice. In addition, a companion volume for salespeople has been developed entitled *Improving Sales Relationships: A Social Styles Approach.** Other resources to aid you in applying the model are listed in Appendix 4 in the back of this book.

Although we each tried to avoid being overly influenced by our own social style, no one can be totally free of style bias. Bob is an Analytical (a C-1 or Driving Analytical); Dot is an Amiable (a

---

*(Cazenovia, N.Y.: Ridge Training Resources, 1984). Available from Ridge Training Resources, 5 Ledyard Avenue, Cazenovia, New York 13035.

C-4 or Expressive Amiable). You probably don't yet know what these words mean, but after reading a bit further, you will discover that this interpersonal shorthand tells you quite a bit about us.

This book was written partly in the quiet of a book-lined study but mainly in the rush and pressure of a busy consulting and training practice. We think this constant interaction between writing and working has made *Social Style/Management Style* more pragmatic.

In this period of transition regarding sexism in language, we know of no option for the use of pronouns that is without problems. Our solution has been to make general references to human beings in feminine terms in the even-numbered chapters and in masculine terms in the odd-numbered chapters.

This book would have been far more difficult to write without the consistent support of our staff. Norma Mierke, our operations manager, runs our organization with unusual efficiency, flexibility, and personal warmth and concern sprinkled with laughter. Liz Smyth punctuates her efficiency in finance and purchasing with adaptability and personal sparkle. Pamela Cahill has brought high energy and commitment to seminar administration and word processing. Hyacinth Brown's and Pat Reakes's varied contributions and Ralph Guldy's maintenance work have kept our conference center and offices pleasant to work and learn in. Chiu Wan Yung provides delicious Chinese and American food at our conference center with unfailing good spirit. While these people only occasionally contributed directly to this book, their support made it possible for us to write it.

Other people on our staff made more direct contributions. Dr. Rick Brandon handles our sales operation and the New York City office with insight, high enthusiasm, and rigorous follow-through. Rick's insights are to be found throughout this book. We've learned much from our thought-provoking trainers—Diane Blecha, Bob Gabor, Larry Kunkel, Marian Lappin-Olson, Tim Timmermann, and Margie Wood. Mike Mullins and Wilma Brownback helped hone the writing. Betsey Bolton read the manuscript several times and made many suggestions that improved the book. We would also like to thank several people at American Management Associations for their contributions: Janet Frick, Rob Kaplan, and Richard Gatjens. Jane Bloom's incisive editing made significant improvements in both the clarity and the readability of the manuscript.

Other than the two of us, the person most responsible for this book's completion is Peg Bates. Her patient typing of drafts and redrafts, and her *un*willingness to type one more revision in the midst of many other pressures, finally made this book a reality.

We hope you'll enjoy and profit from the social style concept as much as we have.

Robert Bolton
Dorothy Grover Bolton
Ridge Conference Center, 1984

Contents

xiii

Contents

PART I

What Is Social Style?

People who have a greater awareness of the communicative significance of actions . . . can be more successful . . . in work that involves the persuasion, leadership, and organization of others. . . . Most can benefit from a greater awareness of their social style, the effect it has on casual and brief interactions with others, or its more general effect on their social life.

—Albert Mehrabian
Silent Messages

CHAPTER 1

Managing Yourself and Working with Others

After reviewing the history of human thought, the philosopher Aldous Huxley said there is only one question of importance: "Who am I and what, if anything, can I do about it?"[1] There are, of course, other basic questions that demand clear answers. For example: "Who are the other people in my life and what, if anything, can I do about the way I interact with them?" Common sense tells us that our answers to these questions will have a major impact on our lives and our work. This book is designed to help you discover pragmatic answers that will contribute to your effectiveness at work and to fulfillment in your life. Our approach is based on the social style concept for understanding oneself and others.

The Social Style Concept

The social style concept, initially formulated by David Merrill and his associates, is perhaps the most useful model for helping people at work understand themselves and others. A social style is a pervasive and enduring pattern of interpersonal behaviors. A more detailed explanation of this concept will be given in the next chapter. For now it is enough to say:

- There are four social styles, none of which is better or worse than any of the other styles.
- Evidence to date suggests that the population of English-speaking Americans is evenly divided (by statistical analysis) among the four styles.
- Each person has a dominant social style, and that style influences the way he works.
- Observable behaviors are the key to understanding a person's social style.
- The best way of discovering one's own social style is to receive feedback from other people.

Understanding Yourself

The most powerful influence on a person's life is the view one holds of oneself. Accurate self-knowledge is essential for:

Developing positive personal relationships.
Managing others effectively.
Setting appropriate life goals and career paths.
Planning and implementing a sound self-improvement program.
Increasing one's creativity.
Increasing other aspects of personal effectiveness.

Self-knowledge is the starting point for effectiveness at work.

Each person has a self-image that, to some degree, does not match reality. A significant difference between self-image and reality can be harmful. The more self-aware you are, the less likely you are to be vulnerable to your illusions. The more aware you are, the more you can do with your life. As our friend Therese Livingstone Smith said, "Awareness is the foundation on which other experiences rest."

In many courses based on the social style concept, each participant receives confidential information about his behavioral patterns from experts on that subject—the people he trusts and who know him well. The feedback received is based on behavior the others observed. This information about how the participant comes across to others is very useful.

Self-knowledge is the starting point of leadership effectiveness. As Machiavelli, the shrewd fifteenth-century author and statesman, wrote, "To lead or attempt to lead without first having a knowledge of self is foolhardy and sure to bring disaster and defeat."[2]

Managing Yourself

Effective self-management is essential to supervising others well. Many management problems that seem to be caused by outside forces actually result from the manager's own behavior. People who try to manage others without first achieving a large measure of self-mastery usually misdirect their energy. As D. H. Lawrence wrote concerning one of his characters, "Poor Richard Lovatt worried himself to death struggling with the problem of himself and calling it Australia."[3] Many a manager has struggled with the problem of himself and called it the department, the boss, or a particular subordinate. As long as a person mismanages himself, he is apt to mismanage everything else.[4]

A central theme of the social style concept is: Excel at being what you are, rather than try to be what you are not. Social style teaching does not suggest that you alter the "essential you." It does not attempt to overhaul you so you will fit some supposedly superior style. Indeed, research shows that every style is effective if it is implemented well and is appropriate to the situation. A major purpose of this book is to help you see the special opportunities and weaknesses of your own managerial style. Then you can capitalize on your strengths and protect yourself against your style-based weaknesses.

Understanding Others

Never before in history have people been required to interact with so many other people. The sheer numbers of people that we have to relate to in the modern organization is a new phenomenon. So, more than ever before, we need an effective way of understanding and working with a wide variety of people. Yet most people find it extremely difficult to understand other people. Lewis Thomas, a gifted and sensitive scientist, said, "Our behavior toward each other is the strangest, most unpredictable, and almost entirely unaccountable of all the phenomena with which we are obliged to live."[5]

There's no question about it: People's behavior is difficult to understand. However, the social style model helps us to see that within a person's seemingly haphazard behavior there is far more order than most people suspect. Much behavior is habitual and fairly predictable. The patterns fall into two crucial dimensions—assertiveness and responsiveness. If you learn to locate a person on these dimensions, you can determine his predominant social style.

Obviously, understanding another person's social style does not tell us all there is to know about that person. But it does give us insight into differences between people and helps us understand some of the potential trouble spots in our relationships with those whose behavior patterns are different from our own. When we lack awareness of another person's working style, it is easy to misconstrue the other's words and behaviors because we often interpret what the other person says and does from the perspective of our own social style rather than the style of the other person.

Understanding other people's social styles improves working relationships by increasing one's acceptance of the other person and his way of doing things. The social style model helps people understand at a deeper level that, just because another person's way of doing the job is different, it isn't necessarily wrong. In fact, each working style, when used effectively and appropriately, can be successful.

Increased acceptance is not only a key to work effectiveness, it is essential for all sound relationships. Philosopher Martin Buber put it this way, "Genuine conversation . . . means acceptance of others."[6]

Working with Others

Although there are other useful applications of social style, the focus of this book is on creating more productive work relationships. This can be partly achieved by factors we have already mentioned:

- Better work relationships begin with improved self-understanding and self-management. Working on a relationship always requires working on oneself.
- Increased understanding and acceptance of others also enhances relationships.

Two other general approaches for improving work relationships are taught in this book. They comprise the principal aspects of what we call "interpersonal flexibility." One of these approaches focuses on the way virtually all people like to be treated. Certain types of interpersonal behavior nearly always work better than others. These basic ways of behaving with people—honestly, fairly, and respectfully—contribute to productive relationships. Without these fundamentals, relationships will be on shaky ground and will usually be exploitive, especially over the long haul.

We use the terms *style flex*[7] and *to flex one's style* to describe the other way of enhancing relationships. It involves the use of interpersonal processes that are compatible with the way the other person chooses to relate. Here, in a nutshell, is how style flex works.

First, identify your own social style. Next, identify the probable social style of the other person. With this information you will be able to predict which aspects of your communication will probably be comfortable for both you and the other person and which aspects may be more strained. You will be able to predict at what points your two styles will mesh and where they are apt to clash. Thus prepared, you can anticipate needless conflicts and miscommunication and head most of them off before they happen. Working with the strengths of others will also become more natural.

Third, having diagnosed the gap between your social style and that of the other person, add or subtract some behaviors from your usual way of relating. That will help the other person feel more comfortable.

Thus, style flex is the temporary use of less habitual behaviors to foster a mutually beneficial interaction. The person who, in addition to treating others honestly, fairly, and with respect, follows these few steps of style flex can increase work effectiveness. Not only can he improve his own performance, but also, through improved work relationships, he can facilitate higher productivity in others.

All of us flex our styles to some degree without even thinking about it. We are more concerned about being on time to a meeting with John, who is known for his punctuality, than with Chris, who seems less time conscious. We are apt to joke for a few minutes before getting down to business with Karen, who loves a good laugh. With Mary, though, we tend to get right to the point because that's the way she prefers to work. When we make these adjustments without thinking about them, we are doing *unconscious* style flex. As a *conscious* approach to work relationships, style flex needs to be done only occasionally—at moments when the stakes are important. To flex one's style all the time would be to lose one's sense of self—probably the greatest loss of all.

The value of interpersonal flexibility is most apparent when compared with its opposite. People with low interpersonal competence tend to withhold or distort important information or to be manipulative. They seek win–lose rather than win–win outcomes. They act in ways that subtly or overtly put themselves up and others down. And they try to force others to work in their own accustomed way rather than adapt their way of working to meet the needs of others.

Management consultant Stuart Atkins says of inflexibility: "My-way-or-your-way is the most tension-producing, dissatisfying, time-wasting, energy-drawing, relationship-breaking activity known to man, woman, or child."[8] Inflexible approaches to people harm relationships and rob us of one of the potentially richest rewards of work life—satisfying human contact. Interpersonal inflexibility also causes productivity to plummet.

Interpersonal Flexibility and Vocational Success

Effectiveness at work has many components. We hardly mention technical ability in this book because our focus is on the interpersonal dimensions. It is obviously important to have the technical skills, but technical mastery alone is insufficient. One needs to be able to relate to others—peers, boss, subordinates, customers, suppliers, regulatory agency personnel, and others. A significant percentage of people who have ample technical skill are hampered by low interpersonal flexibility. Their less-than-adequate ways with people often create needless resistance to them and their ideas. Other factors being equal, the ability to forge productive relationships makes the difference between higher and lower levels of success.

The Interpersonal Factor

Almost all work today involves relating to other people. Studies show that people who have less than the average amount of interpersonal contact at work still spend about 20 percent of their time communicating with others on the job. Usually that fifth of their time is crucial for accomplishing what they want to do. Success or failure in the modern workplace hinges, in large measure, on the effectiveness of interpersonal relationships. For instance, surveys of customers' buying habits reveal the importance of interpersonal competence in that area. In most cases, the customers' decisions to stop buying or to switch to another source is primarily dependent on what salespeople do or don't do to make the buying experience a satisfactory one.

Managers especially find the key responsibility of their position is achieving results with and through other people. Although most managers know this in the top of their minds, on-the-job behavior suggests a very different priority. For instance, when studies in a major chemical company showed that more than half of the managers' work time was spent on people management, the managers' attitude was that their time was being wasted. They didn't think they were being productive unless they were primarily in a doing role rather than in a coaching, facilitating, and coordinating role.[9]

It's not surprising that managers react this way. Early in life they struggle to discover where their aptitude is greatest. Then they discipline themselves in school to develop their areas of skill. During the first years on the job, they further hone those abilities. Then, after one or two promotions, the demands of their jobs change radically. Instead of their chosen areas of concentration, they now need to develop a new specialty—understanding and managing people. Their technical competence may still be important, but if they have several subordinates reporting to them, their most important asset is the ability to achieve productivity through others.

Lasting effectiveness in front-line supervision benefits from interpersonal competence because, in the final analysis, you can manage only with the consent of the managed. People may submit to the exercise of position power for a time, but sooner or later, if that is the supervisor's main source of influence, they will retaliate with strikes, sabotage, or decreased output, or by working elsewhere.

Middle managers must relate effectively both to the upper levels of management and to first- and second-level supervisors. Middle managers also need to relate effectively with peers. Such relationships can be ambiguous and difficult, especially when the peer is crucial to one's goal attainment. Interpersonal skill is essential to high performance in most middle-management positions.

To an even greater degree than in other levels of management, interpersonal competence is needed by executives. Relationships with stockholders, boss, peers, subordinates, and those outside of the organization are varied and demanding. Then, too, many of the most stressful problems in the organization get settled at the highest levels.

A nonprofit research institute studied a group of 21 derailed executives—people who, based on their early successes, were expected to go even higher in the organization but whose progress stalled or whose careers ended when they were fired or forced to retire early. The derailed executives were compared with a group of "arrivers," who made it to the top. These two groups of talented managers showed many similarities and only a few differences. One difference, however, stood out.

> Ability—or inability—to understand other people's perspectives was the most glaring difference between the arrivers and the derailed. Only 25 percent of the derailed were described as having a special ability with people; among the arrivers, the figure was 75 percent.[10]

Just as the primary factor in vocational success is one's ability to work well with people, the reverse is also true. The prime cause of failure in virtually all types of work is unsatisfactory relationships. For decades research aimed at discovering the primary reason for the termination of employees has provided surprisingly consistent results—about 80 percent are fired because of poor interpersonal relationships.

Flexibility and Interpersonal Competence

Of the people important to your success, 75 percent are very different from you. They use time differently, make decisions differently, prefer to relate in different ways, and have different styles of communicating. These differences in style complicate the interpersonal part of our jobs. Part of the problem is that many of us assume that others will react to situations as we would ourselves. But, since three-quarters of the population is different from us, this is unlikely. Style flex provides useful guidelines for dealing with that segment of the population.

David Merrill and Roger Reid conducted research on the relationship of social style and interpersonal versatility to job performance. They found no connection between a person's social style and his job success. On the other hand, they found that what consistently separated the high-performing managers from the low-performing managers was that the more productive managers were rated (by others) as having high interpersonal versatility.[11] Michael Maccoby's study of high-technology companies also links interpersonal flexibility to success.[12]

Our own studies of several organizations show that the average level of flexibility increases at higher levels of the organization. Executives generally have considerably more interpersonal flexibility than is typical in the lower ranks. Obviously, some advocates of a rigid approach to people still make their way to the top ranks of organizations, but the number of inflexibles who are successful seems to be decreasing significantly in the last quarter of this century.

In past decades, low interpersonal flexibility was central to the culture of many industrial organizations. Modern pressures are changing that. We predict that few companies where low flexibility is the norm will survive. American industry needs to face not only the technological challenges of this era but also the interpersonal ramifications of the changes, including the greater need for personnel with high levels of interpersonal flexibility.

To sum up, high interpersonal flexibility is now associated with business success and probably will be an even more important factor in the coming years.

Social Style and
Productive Relationships

In the last half of the twentieth century, it seems especially difficult to establish and maintain significant personal relationships. Divorce statistics combined with research on the failures of many families that do stick together suggest that people need all the help they can get in establishing, restoring, and maintaining close personal ties. There is no panacea for domestic relationships in the 1980s; however, many of our clients tell us that social style methods have helped enormously with their family relationships. Our knowledge of social style has helped us personally through some tough scrapes and enabled us to avoid many others. It has given us many hearty laughs along the way, too. And, as with most people, when our personal relationships thrive, our job performance improves.

Obviously, social style factors are not the only causes of success or failure at work or in other interpersonal situations—not by a long shot. Still, the social style concept is very helpful in creating productive relationships. In the next three chapters, we'll summarize the essential elements of that model. Then, based on that knowledge, the remainder of the book will provide specific information about improving important relationships.

CHAPTER 2

Social Styles

The social style approach to understanding ourselves and others is distinguished from many other models by its emphasis on behavior rather than on personality.[1] Behavior refers to everything a person does that is directly observable. It includes the whole gamut of verbal and nonverbal actions. It is not our purpose to encourage managers and supervisors to become amateur psychologists searching for hidden motivations of co-workers. More harm than help lies on that road. Rather, we focus on how to become better observers of the significant behavioral patterns that are right before our eyes. Since behavior can be seen or heard, our assessments can be confirmed or questioned by other observers.

It is often said that people are like icebergs in that only a fraction of the self is visible on the surface. There are crucial components of each of us that cannot be seen directly—thoughts, motives, feelings, attitudes, values.[2] These important elements of personality can only be inferred (and often incorrectly) from behavior. Much misunderstanding of others comes from guessing at their inner state from their outer behavior. The accompanying cartoon provides one example of how people misread the inner motives from surface behavior.

Social style deals almost exclusively with the surface data of

"No, I'm not seeking political office—I just happen to be good-natured."

people—the tip of the iceberg. These data, though incomplete, are extremely important and are sufficient for most managerial interactions. Supervising behavior rather than the inner world of attitudes and values represents a revolutionary shift for most managers. Few managers are able to report behavior without making inferences about the attitudes behind it. Managers are cautioned against drawing conclusions about motives and personality factors from behavior. In those instances where such judgments are required, they should be made by a sensitive and skilled professional counselor. Peter Drucker is justly emphatic:

> An employer has no business with a man's personality. Employment is a specific contract calling for specific performance, and for nothing else. Any attempt by an employer to go beyond this is usurpation. It is immoral as well

as illegal intrusion of privacy. It is abuse of power. An employee . . . owes performance and nothing else.[3]

Psychologists don't agree as to whether attitudes and values change behavior, or vice versa. It's a "which came first, the chicken or the egg?" type of argument. They do agree to a large extent, however, that when a manager delves into a person's inner world, the manager is acting in ways that are inappropriate and counterproductive. So it is for good reason that the social style model focuses on behavior.

Psychologist Albert Mehrabian emphasizes that individual behaviors can be grouped together in clusters.[4] For example, a person who is perceived as high in assertiveness would exhibit not just one highly assertive behavior but an interrelated pattern of behaviors. Social style is based on the clusters of observable behaviors that people exhibit in interpersonal situations.[5]

What we do when we are alone may be very different from what we do in public.[6] The social style model does not concern itself with solitary behavior—jogging alone, reading, playing solitaire. Social style is about the consistent patterns of actions that a person uses when in the presence of other people.

Two Crucial Behavioral Dimensions

Albert Mehrabian writes:

> There is something about each person, a pervasive style that applies to almost everything he does. . . . Probably it is not just one isolated behavior here or there that gives us an impression but rather a composite of behaviors that are indicative of a certain style. One question, therefore, is "What are these clusters?" or "What are the categories of social behavior?"[7]

Psychologists and leadership and management researchers largely agree that there are two crucial dimensions of interpersonal behavior that determine one's behavioral style.[8] In the social style model these dimensions are labeled "assertiveness" and "responsiveness." The degree to which a person is perceived as being assertive and responsive determines that person's social style.[9]

Assertive Behavior

In the social style model, assertiveness is the degree to which a person's behaviors are seen by others as being forceful or directive. Assertiveness is visualized on a scale divided into four equal segments.[10] The A segment signifies high assertiveness, B means moderately high assertiveness, C represents moderately low assertiveness, and D stands for low assertiveness (see Figure 2-1). Bear in mind that the degree of assertiveness refers to a person's behavior and may not reflect the amount of inner drive.

Each person typically exhibits a cluster of behaviors that fall within one of the segments on the assertion scale. Graphing behavior in this way is useful for analysis, but it does not mean a person's behavior is limited to a single segment of that scale. If you could plot all your interactions with all the people you relate to over time, you would probably find that some behaviors occur in each segment of the assertion scale. Most of your behaviors, however, would cluster in one segment.

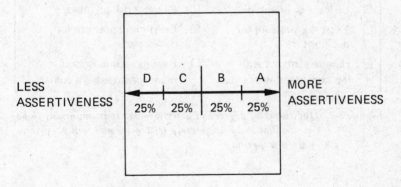

Figure 2-1. The assertiveness scale.

← **LESS
ASSERTIVENESS**

**MORE
ASSERTIVENESS** →

Persons "to the left of the line" tend to:	Persons "to the right of the line" tend to:
☐ Move more slowly and deliberately.	☐ Move more rapidly.
☐ Speak more slowly and more softly.	☐ Speak more quickly, more intensely, and often more loudly.
☐ Lean backward, even when making a request or stating an opinion.	☐ Sit upright or lean forward, especially to make a request or state an opinion.
☐ Be more tentative and less forceful in expressing opinions, making requests, and giving directions.	☐ Be more emphatic when expressing opinions, making requests, and giving directions.
☐ Be less confrontive.	☐ Be more confrontive.
☐ Let others take the interpersonal initiative.	☐ Take the interpersonal initiative.
☐ Be "ask oriented."	☐ Be "tell oriented."
☐ Decide less quickly.	☐ Decide more quickly.
☐ Be less risk oriented.	☐ Be more risk oriented.
☐ Exert less pressure for decisions.	☐ Exert more pressure for decisions.
☐ Have less intense and less consistent eye contact.	☐ Have more intense and more consistent eye contact.

Figure 2-2.   Indicators of degrees of assertiveness. It is important to be aware that these are merely tendencies and will vary from person to person.

You may see yourself moving about the assertion scale rather freely. However, your friends and co-workers will probably see your characteristic behavior in a fairly restricted area of the continuum.

One of the two basic questions we ask in determining a person's social style is: Is the person to the left or the right of the line (the middle point on the scale)? In other words, is the person in the more assertive or less assertive half of the population? The list of indicators in Figure 2-2 will help answer this question.

There is no best place to be on the assertiveness scale. Successful people come from each segment. Participants in our workshops often wonder how less assertive people can be successful. Some people who are low in assertiveness may not get their needs met very often. Some, however, do achieve their goals, through ways that others do not perceive as being directive or forceful. Their determination and drive are exhibited in a more subtle manner.[11]

Responsive Behavior

Responsiveness is defined as the degree to which a person's behaviors are seen by others as being emotionally responsive or expressive, or emotionally controlled (see Figure 2-3). Very responsive people tend to react noticeably to their own emotions or to the emotions of others. Less responsive people are more guarded in their emotional expression.

The second basic question asked in determining a person's social style is: Is the person above or below the line (the middle point on the scale)? In other words, is the person in the more emotionally controlled or the more expressive and responsive part of the population? Figure 2-4 lists some indicators of responsiveness. As with the assertiveness scale, a person's behavior is not limited to a single segment on the responsiveness continuum. But over time, most of a person's behaviors would be seen as clustering in one area. Again, as with assertiveness, there is no best place to be on the responsiveness scale.

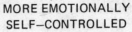

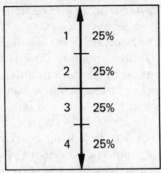

Figure 2-3.   The responsiveness scale.

The Four Social Styles

The two crucial behavioral dimensions form the axes of the social style grid. The four quadrants represent the four social
styles—Analytical, Amiable, Expressive, and Driver (see Figure
2-5).[12] It's important to bear in mind that these styles are neither good nor bad, just different. People from each of the quadrants have achieved impressive successes.

Analytical is the name given to the social style in the upper
left portion of the grid. Analyticals combine a high level of emotional self-control with a low level of assertiveness. Analyticals
tend to take a precise, deliberate, and systematic approach to their
work. They usually gather and evaluate much data before acting. Analyticals are generally industrious, objective, and well-or-
ganized workers.

The *Amiable* social style is located in the lower left quadrant.
Amiables combine higher-than-average responsiveness with a
comparatively low level of assertiveness. They tend to be sym-

LESS RESPONSIVENESS ←	MORE RESPONSIVENESS →
Persons "above the line" tend to:	Persons "below the line" tend to:
☐ Limit their use of gestures.	☐ Gesture more frequently.
☐ Move more rigidly.	☐ Move more freely.
☐ Have less facial expressiveness.	☐ Have more facial expressiveness.
☐ Seem more serious.	☐ Seem more playful.
☐ Appear more reserved.	☐ Appear more friendly.
☐ Dress more formally.	☐ Dress less formally.
☐ Be more controlled in their expression of feelings.	☐ Be freer and less guarded in their expression of feelings.
☐ Focus more on facts.	☐ Focus more on feelings.
☐ Appear more task oriented than people oriented.	☐ Appear more people oriented than task oriented.
☐ Be less interested in small talk, anecdotes, and jokes.	☐ Be more interested in small talk, anecdotes, and jokes.
☐ Make decisions based more on facts than on emotions.	☐ Allow feelings to have a greater influence on decision making.
☐ Demonstrate more discipline in their use of time.	☐ Demonstrate less structure in their use of time.
☐ Supervise in a more disciplined manner.	☐ Supervise in a more personal manner.

Figure 2-4.   Indicators of degrees of responsiveness. These are tendencies that will vary from person to person.

pathetic to the needs of others and are often quite sensitive to what lies below the surface behavior of another person. Of all the social styles, Amiables are most likely to use empathy and understanding in interpersonal problem solving. The Amiables' trust in other people may bring out the best in their customers, friends, and subordinates.

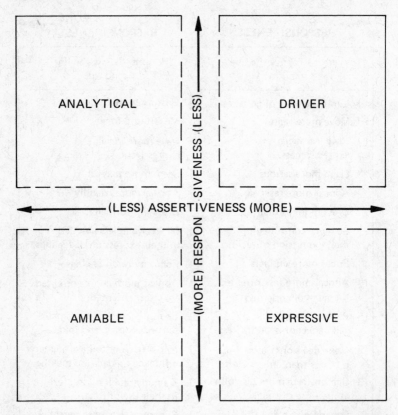

Figure 2-5.   The social style grid. The axes are formed by the two be-
havioral dimensions; the quadrants represent the four social
styles.

The *Expressives,* the most flamboyant social style, are found
in the lower right area of the grid. They integrate a high level
of assertiveness with much emotional expression. Expressives
tend to look at the big picture, often take fresh, novel approaches to problems, and are willing to take risks in order to
seize opportunities and realize their dreams. Their love of fun,
use of humor, and spontaneous ways often lift the morale of their

co-workers. The expressive's ability to charm, persuade, excite, and inspire people with a vision of the future can be a strong motivating force. Expressives tend to decide and act quickly.

The *Driver* social style is located in the upper right section of the grid. Drivers blend a high level of emotional self-control with a high degree of assertiveness. They are task-oriented people who know where they are going and what they want. They get to the point quickly and express themselves succinctly. Drivers are typically pragmatic, decisive, results oriented, objective, and

Different management styles can produce the same favorable results.

competitive. They are usually independent, willing to take sound risks, and valued for their ability to get things done.

Figure 2-6 provides a summary of some of the strengths of each social style. Since there is no best place to be on either the assertiveness or the responsiveness scale, logic suggests that no one social style is better than any other. Remember, successful managers and salespersons are found in all four social styles.[13] Figures 2-7 and 2-8 show famous people of each social style.

A person's working style is usually an outgrowth of her social

ANALYTICAL	DRIVER
LOGICAL	INDEPENDENT
THOROUGH	CANDID
SERIOUS	DECISIVE
SYSTEMATIC	PRAGMATIC
PRUDENT	EFFICIENT
AMIABLE	EXPRESSIVE
COOPERATIVE	OUTGOING
SUPPORTIVE	ENTHUSIASTIC
DIPLOMATIC	PERSUASIVE
PATIENT	FUN LOVING
LOYAL	SPONTANEOUS

Figure 2-6.   Some strengths of each social style.

Culver Pictures

The Granger Collection, New York

RCA Records and Tapes

The Granger Collection, New York

Figure 2-7. Public figures from each social style: Albert Einstein (Analytical), Mike Wallace (Driver), John Denver (Amiable), and Liza Minnelli (Expressive).

FAMOUS ANALYTICALS	FAMOUS DRIVERS
Jimmy Carter	Henry Ford I
Albert Einstein	Barbara Walters
Woodrow Wilson	Malcolm X
Eleanor Roosevelt	Charles Lindbergh
Thomas Jefferson	Mike Wallace
FAMOUS AMIABLES	FAMOUS EXPRESSIVES
Gerald Ford	Liza Minnelli
John Denver	Winston Churchill
Dwight Eisenhower	Muhammad Ali
Mary Tyler Moore	Franklin D. Roosevelt
Robert E. Lee	Pablo Picasso

Figure 2-8.   Some successful people from each social style.

style. If a person's management style differs significantly from her social style, that person is probably managing outside her comfort zone and will not utilize her capacities to the fullest. Further, excessive stress results from operating with a working style different from one's dominant social style.

The effective organization is made up of and values all four types of managers. According to management consultant Peter Drucker, "The top-management tasks require at least four different kinds of human beings: the 'thought man' [Analytical], the 'action man' [Driver], the 'people man' [Amiable], and the 'front man' [Expressive]."[14] Drucker points out that you are unlikely to find all the strengths of all four types in any one manager.

Characteristic Weaknesses of Each Style

In addition to its strengths, each social style has characteristic weaknesses. One way of looking at these weaknesses is that a given social style tends to be less developed in the areas in which the other styles are strong. Normally a person is especially lacking in the strengths of the style diagonally across the grid from her own style. Supportiveness is one of the Amiable's greatest strengths; it is usually one of the Driver's weak points. Contagious enthusiasm, a strength of Expressives, is rarely an asset of an Analytical. The objectivity of a Driver may be lacking in an Amiable. The precision of the Analytical is seldom well developed in an Expressive.

On the other hand, some of the most serious weaknesses of a social style result from overextending the style's strengths. This notion burst forcefully into the mind of management consultant Paul Mok as he was enjoying a hot summer day on Connecticut's Lordship Beach reading Alexander Dumas's *The Count of Monte Cristo*. Suddenly he came across Dumas's line, "Any virtue carried to the extreme can become a crime." Mok suddenly realized:

> All of these hundreds of executives whom I've counseled over the years were having interpersonal problems not because of their weaknesses, but because of their strengths. They were over-using their strengths, employing them even when they were inappropriate, using them to the hilt—and beyond. And when used to excess, these strengths backfired—exploded in their faces.

STYLE	STRENGTHS		OVEREXTENDED
Analytical	Precise	➡	Nit-picking
	Systematic	➡	Inflexible
Amiable	Supportive	➡	Conforming
	Easygoing	➡	Permissive
Expressive	Enthusiastic	➡	Overbearing
	Imaginative	➡	Unrealistic
Driver	Determined	➡	Domineering
	Objective	➡	Unfeeling

Figure 2-9.   Strengths of a style become weaknesses when overextended.

Figure 2-9 notes how the strengths of each style can become weaknesses when overextended.

The overextension of strengths also causes managerial ineffectiveness. The Analytical's quest for quality is misused when she spends additional time to get better-than-needed quality on a low-priority item while more important matters are left unattended. The Driver's push for short-term results is inappropriate when it forfeits greater long-range gain. The Expressive's big-picture dreams can be a detriment if they prevent her from doing the nitty-gritty that must be done daily. The Amiable's supportiveness can be a weakness when she refuses to challenge a course of action she believes will have a negative impact on the organization.

The wise manager capitalizes on her strengths and develops strategies for minimizing the damage caused by her weaknesses.

CHAPTER 3

Most Commonly Asked Questions about Social Style

As we've taught the social style model to managers, hundreds of questions have been raised. Most, however, are variations of the five questions discussed in this chapter.

How Can I Really Have One Social Style When I Behave Differently in Different Situations?

Our definition of social style states that a person's style is "a pervasive . . . pattern of interpersonal behaviors." According to one dictionary, the word *pervasive* means *spread throughout*. A person's social style is his characteristic way of behaving across a variety of situations. Social style influences nearly everything a person does with other people.

In response to this kind of statement, people often tell us that they and others behave in very different ways, depending on the situation. They behave one way at work, another way with their families, and still differently when bowling or playing tennis with friends. The study of scholars also supports the belief that people's behavior is often altered when circumstances change. Psychologist William James claimed each person has "as many social selves as there are distinct groups of persons about whose opinion he cares."[1] And management expert Edgar Schein writes, "The roles which people occupy partly determine how they will behave."[2] Role relationships of boss–subordinate, boss–secretary, teacher–pupil, parent–child, husband–wife, and so forth tend to be somewhat stereotyped. As we move from role to role, our behavior can be expected to change.

It is not surprising, then, that managers often ask us how these situational differences in behavior can be reconciled with the statement that one's social style tends to express itself across a variety of situations.

More and Less Variable Kinds of Behavior

Some types of behavior change considerably from one situation to another; other types change less. Psychological researcher John Geier writes, "Some aspects of the person's style remain stable; these personality traits are present regardless of the change in social field. These traits are termed field-invariant. But a number of behaviors are determined by the social field."[3] While people may act somewhat differently from one situation to another, behaviors associated with assertiveness and responsiveness seem to stay fairly consistent,[4] and although some behaviors do change, a person's dominant social style tends to remain the same.

Four-Style People

We are not saying, however, that the dominant behavior is used inevitably. The social style model holds that we are all four-style people. No person ever conforms completely to one type.[5] On the other hand, virtually everyone has one style that predominates, one that is used most frequently.[6] This is the style with which the person feels most comfortable. It is the style that tends to require the least amount of energy and usually generates the least stress for the person.

How Can You Say a Person Isn't Likely to Change His Style?

Some managers tell us very insistently that people can change, and they report significant changes in their own lives.[7] Experts add their testimony. For example, philosopher William Hocking declares:

> Of all animals, it is man in whom heredity counts for least, and conscious building forces for most. Consider that his infancy is longest, his instincts least fixed, his brain most unfinished at birth, his powers of habit-making and habit-changing most marked, his susceptibility to social impressions keenest. . . . To everyone who asserts as dogma that 'Human nature never changes,' it is fair to reply, 'It is human nature to change itself.'[8]

So, in virtually every workshop we conduct, managers wonder, "How can you say a person isn't likely to change his social style?"

There is a certain irony about the question because there is no best style. Yet, at the beginning of our seminars, people still think that there are better and worse styles. Other people who are aware that all styles are equally good would, for variety's sake, prefer to try out a different social style for a while. For one reason or another the question continually crops up. It is in part a reaction to the definition, which states "social style is [an] *enduring* pattern of interpersonal behavior." That is, once established, one's dominant style remains dominant throughout life.[9]

We both asked that question, too, and sought evidence from the lives of acquaintances and historical characters that a person can indeed change his social style. Our conclusion surprised us. Among the normal population, there is no one we know personally and no one we know of in history whose social style has changed.[10] We've searched for exceptions but haven't found any yet.

One person who seemed to change her social style was a Driver until retirement; then she appeared to become an Amiable. But when we examined her behavior further, we found she was still as high on assertiveness as ever. As a senior citizen, the assertive behaviors weren't focused on work goals but on her new life interest—doing activities with other people. She organized fellow retirees to go on trips and was president of various gray-power citizen organizations. Her emotional control remained strong, too. Although she spent much more time with people in her retirement, she was still activity oriented. While displaying more warmth in her interactions, she was still quite emotionally controlled. She was still a Driver.

The Large Patterns of Continuity

The three founding fathers of modern psychiatry were very conscious of the large patterns of continuity that are woven in our past and continue into our future. Sigmund Freud taught that "the essential foundations of character are laid down by the age of three and . . . later events can modify but not alter the traits then established."[11] Alfred Adler, who disagreed with Freud on so many things, dates the adaptation of a permanent life-style at age four or five.[12] Carl Jung assumed that some basic tendencies of a person's psychological type are part of his genetic inheritance.[13] As far as we can tell, one's social style is part of those unchanging patterns of continuity.

This is not an irrelevant side issue. Since you probably can't change them, accepting your social style and the styles of the people you work with is a key to effectiveness. When you work within your style—your habitual way of behaving—there is an immense economy of energy if your style-based behaviors are appropriate to the situation. It is a comparatively effortless way of operating.

The Inevitability of Change

When people hear us say that social style probably can't be changed, they often interpret that to mean people can't change at all. That's not what we mean. People change continually. While you can't change your basic style, you can develop:

- The strengths of your dominant style.[14]
- Your ability to capitalize on style-based strengths.
- Your ability to protect yourself from consequences of style-based weaknesses.
- Strengths that are characteristic of other styles (without trying to switch styles).[15]
- Your ability to flex your style to improve relationships.

The "law of change" says that if we are not growing we are regressing. This book and the workshops we teach are part of our effort to facilitate growth—that is, positive change—in ourselves and others. The social style model helps you channel your self-improvement efforts into areas where they can be fruitful.

Doesn't Social Style Ignore the Uniqueness of Individuals?

Some managers are concerned that the social style model will take the focus off the individual in the workplace. One of the most effective ways of exploiting people has been to depersonalize them and place them in categories. Since the early days of the industrial revolution, some managers have thought of their workers as factory hands, not individuals. By categorizing them in that way, managers no longer had to treat them as people, let alone as unique human beings.

Sensitive managers often wonder whether the social style model isn't just one more way of depersonalizing people. Deep ethical concern often lies behind their question: "Doesn't social style ignore the uniqueness of individuals?" This question penetrates to the core of one of the potential dangers of the social style model.

Our answer is: "Yes, the social style model deliberately ignores individual differences."[16] We add, however, that some method of categorization that overlooks individual differences is inevitable. Finally, we suggest that managers use what we call Korzybski's Solution (discussed later) to minimize this serious problem.

Three Perspectives on People

Each person is in some ways:

Like all other people.
Like no other person.
More like some people than others.

These three perspectives can help us arrive at a better understanding of ourselves and others.

First, in certain respects, everyone is like all other people. *Homo sapiens* constitutes a species and can be distinguished from other species. People are not mistaken for apes or elephants, canaries or crocodiles. Characteristics of behavior as well as physical indicators distinguish human beings as a species. Humans have a lot in common, but it is also true that in some ways each of us is unique. Your fingerprints are distinct from those of every other person who ever lived. Experts can distinguish your voice from that of all others. These are merely surface indicators of a more significant truth. At birth, you were endowed with an individuality of personhood that can never be copied and can never be fully eradicated. Both of these perspectives on people are extremely important. It is folly to ignore either of them.

The third perspective is intended to be a supplement to, rather than a replacement for, the other two ways of thinking about people. It is with this third perspective that social style concerns itself: In some significant ways, each of us is more like some people than others. In other words, social style is a way of categorizing people. We have provided some aids for integrating these three perspectives (Korzybski's Solution and the approaches suggested in Chapter 10, for example).

People Inevitably Think in Categories

Anthropologist and linguist Peter Farb states, "Everyone, whether he realizes it or not, classifies the items he finds in his environment."[17] This tendency is essential for survival and begins at a very early age. Infants begin to sort the confusing array of objects they encounter into classifications that are helpful to them. They distinguish between foods and not-foods, persons and not-persons, moving objects and not-moving objects. These simple generalizations help the infant predict what to expect and thus to survive.

We rely on classifications for two reasons. First, to learn about one specimen is to learn something about all of them. Given the number of separate objects each person encounters in a day, classification is an essential economy.[18] Second, classification enables us to predict what this type of object can be expected to do.[19] Being able to tell a rattler from a nonpoisonous snake at a distance can be a helpful guide to action in some parts of the country.

To exist, people have to think in categories. Since we live in an interpersonal environment, we inevitably categorize people. Many of the categories are inaccurate and not very useful. The most viable option we have is to use the best possible categories. Our experience suggests that the social style model provides the most accurate and useful categories for many managerial interactions.[20]

While categorization is inevitable and can be useful, it can also be badly misused. People often forget that their method of classifying people into types is only one of three perspectives on people. The "If you know one, you know 'em all" approach hinders understanding, whether the categories are labor–management, black–white, male–female, or Analytical–Expressive.

Korzybski's Solution

Alfred Korzybski, a Polish-American scientist, proposed a solution to the problem caused by our need to categorize and the danger of overlooking individual characteristics.[21] S. I. Hayakawa summarizes:

> It is the suggestion made by Korzybski that we add "index numbers" to our terms, thus: $Englishman_1$, $Englishman_2$, $Englishman_3$ . . . ; cow_1, cow_2, cow_3 . . . ; $Frenchman_1$, $Frenchman_2$, $Frenchman_3$ . . . ; $communist_1$, $communist_2$, $communist_3$. . . . The terms of the classification tell us what the individuals in that class have in common; the index numbers remind us of the characteristics left out. A rule can then be formulated as a general guide in all our thinking and reading: Cow_1 is not cow_2; Jew_1 is not Jew_2; $politician_1$ is not $politician_2$; and so on. This rule, if remembered, prevents us from confusing levels of abstraction and forces us to consider the facts on those occasions when we might otherwise find ourselves leaping to conclusions which we might later have cause to regret.[22]

In social style terms, it is very important to remember that one Amiable is not the same as another Amiable, nor is one Driver the same as another Driver. Appendix 3 describes some differences within a given social style.

How Can You Assume That Outer Behavior Matches the Person's Inner Being?

Some managers tell us that appearances can be deceiving. They say behavioral patterns can be a facade that hides the inner person. Someone who is insecure may swagger precisely because he is insecure. A person who acts laid back may be far more purposeful than he seems. Centuries ago Confucius pointed to this type of discrepancy:

> Man's mind is . . . more difficult to know than the sky. For
> with the sky you know what to expect with respect to the
> coming of spring, summer, autumn and winter, and the al-
> ternation of day and night. But man hides his character be-
> hind an inscrutable appearance.[23]

Novels often note the contrast between outer behavior and inner feeling. D. H. Lawrence describes an interaction between
two sisters. After twice being slapped on the face by her sister,
"Ursula with *boiling* heart went meekly away."[24] Dostoevsky
describes two brothers, one an Expressive and the other an
Amiable, whose behaviors were incredibly different even when
their inner feelings were virtually the same.[25]

All of us have sensed times when the outward and the inward
persons were in stark contradiction to one another. Thus the
question, "How can you assume that outer behavior matches the
person's inner being?" The answer is, we don't make that assumption. On the contrary, the social style model is based on
the assumption that there is often a significant discrepancy between inner reaction and outer response. In reaction to a specific situation, an Analytical may experience as much emotional
intensity as an Expressive. The Expressive's behavior, however,
will typically demonstrate more feeling. Merrill and Reid com-
ment:

> The person who appears warm and friendly may not, in fact,
> like us any more than the one who appears serious and de-
> tached. Similarly, the dynamic, forceful-appearing individ-
> ual may not . . . believe in [his idea] as strongly as the quiet,
> less assuming one. These labels ["assertiveness" and "re-
> sponsiveness"] do not define what a person is thinking or
> feeling; they only describe aspects of observable behavior.[26]

Now you may wonder how a model based on observable behavior is very useful if inner and outer behavior do not match.
We have three responses to this. First, the social style model
would probably be far more useful if behavior always revealed a
person's inner world. Second, no one has direct access to an-

other person's inner world; our only valid clues about the person stem from his behavior. That's all the information we have to work with. Therefore, if a model won't work simply because it is based on behavior, no model for improving relationships will work. Finally, it has been our experience that the social style model does work. It helps us make fairly accurate predictions about how others will behave. And its prescriptions for constructive responses have proven very productive. The acid test of this model is your use of it in your relationships.

How Can I Be Sure of My Own Social Style?

This question doesn't occur very often in our workshops, since all participants receive feedback on how other people perceive their social styles. Before the course begins, participants are asked to select several people who know them well and whose opinions they respect. These people complete a confidential inventory about the participant. This is not a test that you pass or fail. It is a method carefully developed by experts in the field to provide feedback on how a person comes across to others. Computer-tabulated responses produce a composite picture of the primary social style projected by the participant. For most participants, a high point in the workshop occurs when they receive this feedback on their social styles. It serves as a foundation for self-development and for improving work relationships.

You are probably wondering how you can be sure of your own social style if you do not attend such a workshop. This is a problem because self-assessment is not apt to be very reliable. According to our experience in conducting workshops, a person has about a 50 percent likelihood of assessing his own style correctly.

Two behavioral scientists, Joseph Luft and Harry Ingham, have convincingly demonstrated that all of us are, in significant but varying degrees, unaware of how we are perceived by others.[27]

In many ways we do not see ourselves as others do. As often is the case, the poets reached that insight long ago. Robert Burns, the Scottish bard, wrote:

O wad some Pow'r the giftie gie us,
To see oursel's as ithers see us!
It wad frae monie a blunder free us,
   An' foolish notion: [28]

ANALYTICAL	DRIVER
Less Assertiveness and Less Responsiveness	More Assertiveness and Less Responsiveness
AMIABLE	EXPRESSIVE
Less Assertiveness and More Responsiveness	More Assertiveness and More Responsiveness

Figure 3-1. Chart for recording feedback on how others perceive your assertiveness and responsiveness.

How can you get an accurate assessment of your social style? As we've mentioned, attending a course that uses a sound instrument is one way.* If that option is out, your best bet is to ask three to five acquaintances to provide you with feedback by choosing, from each of the paired indicators in Figures 2-2 and 2-4, the one that more accurately applies to you. Then, when you have compiled those data, place a checkmark in the appropriate quadrant in Figure 3-1.

We have one more aspect of the social style model to explore before examining applications to interpersonal relationships. The next chapter focuses on the backup styles people tend to use when they experience excessive stress.

---

*There are only a few instruments that, by our standards, are fairly sound. Most professionals who use these instruments will make them available only in a training or counseling session. For information about how to be trained in the use of a social style feedback instrument, write Ridge Consultants, 5 Ledyard Avenue, Cazenovia, N.Y. 13035. The training we provide is rigorous.

CHAPTER 4

Backup Styles: Responses to Excess Stress

Two facts about stress are abundantly clear. First, most people experience considerable stress at work. Second, under excess stress a person's behavior tends to change. This chapter describes backup styles—predictable, style-based behavioral changes in response to stress.

Fight or Flight

The "dean" of stress research, Hans Selye, conducted nearly 40 years of investigation on the stress of life. These years of study convinced him that there are only two basic reactions available for coping with stress. A person can respond "actively, through fight, or passively, by running away or putting up with it. . . . The degree to which various people get satisfaction from active or passive behavior differs enormously."[1]

The social style backup model parallels Selye's findings. Merrill and Reid and their associates found that the more assertive

41

styles (Drivers and Expressives) tend to become more active and more aggressive when they are under pressure. By contrast, the less assertive styles (Amiables and Analyticals) tend to appear more passive. It has also been discovered that, under stress, people who are high on responsiveness (Amiables and Expressives) tend to exaggerate some of their style-based characteristics associated with responsiveness. Likewise, Analyticals and Drivers, under pressure, are apt to emphasize some of their style-based tendencies related to control of emotional expression.[2]

The concept of primary backup styles is based on these predictable shifts of behavior in response to stress.

Primary Backup Styles

A person's primary backup style is her predictable, unconscious shift of behavior to more extreme, rigid, and nonnegotiable forms in response to a high level of stress. Backup behavior is usually counterproductive for the person using it and very hard on her relationships. Let's explore some key ideas in this definition.

First, backup style is the pattern of behaviors a person uses when confronted with *a high level of stress*.[3] These behaviors offer a way of focusing on personal needs and relieving tension, although at the same time they tend to increase other people's stress. Backup behavior isn't the only way of relieving tension, but it takes the least effort initially and often provides quick relief.

When a person is in backup style, a shift to more extreme forms of behavior has occurred. As we have seen, people under stress tend to move further out on the assertiveness and responsiveness scales. Behaviors characteristic of their dominant style are exaggerated and their strengths are transformed into weaknesses.

Backup behavior is *rigid*.[4] It is a response more to the pressure inside the person than to what the interpersonal situation calls for. Thus, backup behavior is usually also inappropriate.

When in primary backup, a person takes a *nonnegotiable* stance in terms of the way she will interact with people. Regardless of the needs of other people, the demands of the situation, or any other factors, the person tends to interact in her characteristic way and no other. The my-way-not-your-way aspect of backup behavior produces major strains on relationships.

The shift from social style to primary backup style is usually made *without conscious choice.* It occurs without thought or premeditation. Further, backup behavior is *predictable.* Persons of the same social style tend to have the same primary backup pattern.

Finally, backup behavior is usually *counterproductive.* Extreme, rigid, and nonnegotiable behavior is tough on relationships. It undermines motivation; raises other people's stress, thereby undercutting their productivity; and may ultimately generate more stress for the person exhibiting the backup behavior.

Some backup behavior is inevitable, but too much of it is self-defeating. In his book *Self-Realization and Self-Defeat,* psychologist Samuel Warner describes the effects of what we call backup behavior: "Behavior may be *adjustive* without being *adaptive* [Warner's emphasis]. That is, behavior may permit anxiety reduction without in the least assisting the individual's long term welfare. It may even be seriously injurious to it."[5]

Each social style has its own primary backup style.[6] The Driver becomes autocratic, the Expressive attacking, the Analytical avoiding, and the Amiable acquiescing (see Figure 4-1).[7]

When in backup style, the Driver tends to become pushy and dictatorial. Because she becomes more emotionally controlled, instead of shouting to get her way, she may speak in a level but intense voice while riveting you with cold, insistent, unyielding eyes. In backup style, the Driver often becomes even more task oriented, insisting that things be done her way and right now. Some Drivers, like Lucy in the accompanying comic strip, show more emotion than others when they are in backup.

Under an overload of tension, the Expressive—unlike the

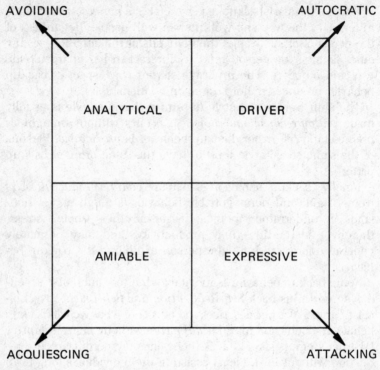

Figure 4-1. Primary backup styles.

Driver, who may stay task oriented when in backup—typically unleashes an angry personal attack, using strong language, high volume, and emphatic gestures.

When Amiables move into backup they usually acquiesce. Although genuinely supportive under normal circumstances, the Amiable in backup tends to offer compliance rather than cooperation. Under backup conditions, the Amiable's heart is not in the consent that is communicated. Although she acquiesces, she may not do what she agrees to.

An Analytical becomes an avoider when in backup. The Analytical may even leave the room physically. What is more com-

mon, however, is vacating the scene emotionally. When an Analytical in backup doesn't leave the room or sulk in silence, she
will tend to intellectualize and discuss emotional issues with a
cold and detached logic. She doesn't let others know, and may
not even know herself, that she is churning inside.

Sometimes a person moves into backup style instantaneously.
At other times, the process is slow and gradual. One of the authors, for example, is an Amiable whose supportiveness is genuine most of the time. It has taken both of us quite a while to
be able to detect early on when she begins to slip into the acquiescing mode. She may say the agreeable words, but there is
a slight difference in her tone of voice, facial expressions, and
so forth. The words are the same, but not the music.

Second, Third, and Fourth Backup Styles

When people move into backup style, their own tension is usually reduced and they then return to their more normal range of
behaviors. If, however, the tension continues to build, the person will probably move into a second backup style, across the
assertion scale.[8] That is, if fight behaviors don't work, people tend
to revert to flight and vice versa. Thus a Driver, after becoming
autocratic, may move across the assertion scale and become
avoiding (see Figure 4-2). If the tension becomes still greater,
she moves diagonally across the grid into a third backup style,
attacking. While it rarely happens, if a Driver still finds no tension release, she moves back across the assertion continuum into
a fourth backup style—she acquiesces.

The pattern of backup behaviors for each social style is shown
in Figure 4-3. Many, but certainly not all, people follow this typical pattern.

All social style predictions are probabilities, and this is especially true of backup patterns. The important point is that you
probably do have some backup pattern, as do your friends and
associates. If you can recognize your pattern and the patterns of
others, you can avoid much needless and harmful friction.

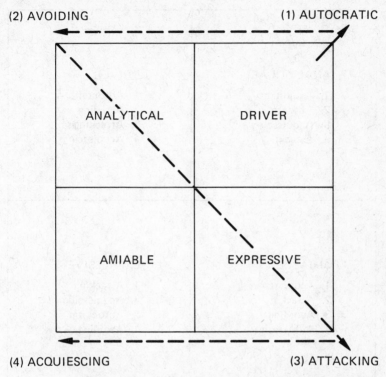

Figure 4-2. Under extreme stress, a person of any social style may experience four sequential backup styles. A Driver's successive backup tendencies are diagrammed here.

The Vicious Circle

People of one style of behavior can rub people of another style the wrong way. You can imagine how much more stress can be triggered in a relationship when you are in your backup style, using behaviors that are extreme, rigid, and nonnegotiable. When one person is in backup, she tends to push others into backup, and a vicious circle of increasingly antagonistic transactions tends

Figure 4-3.   Backup behaviors for each social style.

to occur. As the interpersonal conflict rises, productivity plummets.

When an Analytical in backup acts emotionally detached, she usually generates annoyance in other people. As an Expressive said, "I can deal with hate, I can deal with anger, I can deal with despair, I can deal with anybody that is feeling anything, but I can't deal with *nothing*."[9] If an Expressive in backup uses her tongue to wound, she is apt to trigger backup behavior in others. When a Driver uses power to control others autocratically, she may find the victims using more extreme, rigid, and nonnegotiable behavior. When an Amiable becomes artificially agreeable, tension in others usually rises noticeably. Whatever your backup behaviors, they are liable to trigger a spiral of increasing stress in your relationships that lowers productivity in the short run. If used too often, those behaviors can have negative effects for the long haul as well.

In the following chapters, we'll show you how to be yourself while at the same time adapting to other people's style-based ways of relating. We call this style flex. Then in Chapter 9, with an understanding of style flex as a background, we will discuss ways of coping with your own and other people's backup behavior.

PART II

Interpersonal Flexibility

All of us have a large repertory of possible roles and behavioral styles to bring into play in any given situation.

—Edgard Schein
Process Consultation: Its Role in Organizational Development

CHAPTER 5

Style Flex: Building Bridges, Not Boxes

Much of the miscommunication and many of the conflicts that occur at work are style based.[1] When participants in our courses become aware of this, they are quick to see that style flex is one of the most productive applications of the social style model.[2] Although it has not always been called the same thing, the concept of style flex has been around for a long time. Socrates said that the person who would persuade others (the orator) must understand the basic categories of people and know what approach works best with each type.[3]

In this chapter we will define style flex, note when to use it, and explore two common concerns about it.

What Is Style Flex?

Style flex is doing what is appropriate for the situation by temporarily using some behaviors typical of one's nondominant social styles. Let's look at each part of this definition.

Doing what is appropriate is the essence of style flex. The person who uses style flex well reads situations accurately and responds in ways that are fitting. You can gauge whether your behavior is appropriate for the interaction by monitoring the other person's stress level. Appropriate behavior usually reduces the tension of the other person.

Two types of variables influence the typical managerial situation—human factors and nonhuman factors. In this book we focus primarily on the human factors. It is important, however, not to overlook the nonhuman factors; sometimes these factors are more significant than the interpersonal ones.[4]

Technology, the way a person's work is done, should influence the person's behavioral approach to some situations. The organization's goals, structure, policies, norms, and climate also help define what is or is not appropriate. In addition, such external factors as economic, political, social, and cultural influences often contribute to a person's understanding of the situation. A Driver interacting with an Analytical might flex his style differently during an idea-generating discussion than in a crisis-ridden production situation. In order to avoid short-term solutions, it is helpful to take a step back and see things in their larger context.[5]

The word *temporarily* is significant, because most of the time it is inappropriate to consciously flex one's style. Yet there will be crucial moments nearly every day when it is desirable to act in harmony with the behavior of another person's dominant style and other situational factors.

Style flex also involves behavior. Management consultant Peter Honey states:

> Behavior is critical in human relationships precisely because it is the part of us that is readily evident to other people. Their attitudes toward us and, more importantly, their behavior toward us are largely determined by our behavior toward them. This interaction between people's behavior is important because it in large part affects what is achieved or not achieved.[6]

Style flex is a way of taking responsibility for the results you achieve through your behavior. It is communicating in a way more readily understood by and more agreeable to persons of another social style. It involves using some body language and wording that match the preference of the person whose style you are flexing to. In Chapter 7 we specify types of nonverbal behavior and uses of language that are often appropriate for people of specific social styles.

Many people misconstrue style flex. They think of it as radically changing behavior when with another person. However, such extreme and widespread changes are apt to damage a relationship and are not what we mean by style flex. Style flex assumes that you will accent many of the behaviors you have in common with the other person.[7] There are a lot of preferences that the two of you share. Be sure you draw on those ways of relating that overlap with the preferences of the other person.

Another aspect of style flex is to select a few types of behaviors that you will add to or subtract from your usual repertoire. For example, a Driver in relating to an Amiable decided to alter his usual behavior in three ways. He consciously spoke more slowly and left more periods of silence in the conversation. He invited the Amiable to state his opinions while he himself refrained from judging any part of what the Amiable said until he fully understood the whole idea. Finally, the Driver stated his opinions less forcefully than usual. According to the Driver who described the interaction to us, those few changes in behavior contributed to the most productive interchange he had ever had with the Amiable peer, whose cooperation is essential to the Driver's success.

Style flex does not mean giving up your goals. Rather, it means working toward goals in ways that are more comfortable to a person of a different social style. If style flex is not likely to make things better, don't use it.[8]

Many people find it difficult to distinguish between *content* (what they are trying to achieve) and *process* (how they go about trying to achieve it).[9] Style flex is the employment of appropriate interpersonal processes to achieve desirable outcomes.

When to Flex Your Style

In general, it is appropriate to flex your style whenever it is needed to establish and maintain mutually productive relationships. Four guidelines are discussed below.

- *Not all the time.* The person who tries to flex his style all the time undermines his own personality: "To be always 'on'" would be to destroy ourselves."[10] Important as style flex is, it is also important to express one's personality, including the use of one's own style-based behavior. It is a waste to be created unique only to become a mere bundle of responses to random stimuli.

Ironically, people who overdo style flex are not trusted. Rensis Likert, a noted researcher of supervisory practices, says:

> Some supervisors, for example, are more outgoing and ex-troverted, others quieter and more reserved. Subordinates come to expect the supervisor to behave in a manner consistent with his personality. Supervisory acts and the ways of expressing one's self which are appropriate for one kind of supervisor may be quite inappropriate for another. When a supervisor behaves in ways which do not fit his personality, his behavior is apt to communicate to his subordinates something quite different from what the supervisor intends. Subordinates usually view such behavior with suspicion and distrust.[11]

Using style flex too often can be as detrimental as not using it enough. As with all things, there is a time, a place, and a degree for the effective use of style flex.

- *When something important is at stake.* Style flex is most frequently used when there is something important you want to accomplish. When you are meeting with a major customer, when you are making a request for an increased budget or additional personnel, when you are meeting with an official from a regulatory agency—these are examples of times to use style flex. It can be very helpful when you or the other person are trying to achieve a significant objective.

- *When the other person is stressed.* Many people operate under excessive stress much of the time. When you see signs of high stress in another person, use style flex to avoid generating additional tension that could send that person into backup behavior.

■ *To get off on the right foot.* The beginning of a conversation is often very stressful for people and frequently sets the tone for the rest of the interaction. This is a time for building rapport. One way of doing that is to identify the other person's social style and "open in parallel"—that is, adopt a similar style at the beginning of the conversation. In the opening minutes, try to help the other person feel comfortable. Obviously, if you interact with someone several times a day, you do this on a selective basis.

People often remember to open in parallel with the bigwigs in their company, with customers, and with important strangers, but what a revolution in work relationships would result if, once a day, each of us opened in parallel with our subordinates and peers and what a transformation of family life if we did this with our spouses, children, and parents.

Even in the most difficult interpersonal situations at work, such as a tough performance review, you'll rarely need to spend as much as an hour a day flexing your style. Even so, it can be one of your most significant management resources if, when you do use style flex, it is at the crucial moments in your work or personal life, the times that are essential to your effectiveness, and it will help significantly with the daily maintenance of relationships that counts for so much over time.

Two Concerns about Style Flex

People in our workshops raise two objections to style flex. Let's take a look at them before learning how style flex works.

"I Don't Want to Be Phony"

Some people believe that flexing one's style inevitably means not being oneself. And it is true that some people do seem phony when they flex their style. However, these are people who, rather than following the guidelines we suggest, often try to flex too much and too often. It is important to remember that interpersonal flexibility, as we define it, includes treating people honestly, fairly, and respectfully. Building on that base, style flex is a sincere effort to help the other person relate to you in ways comfortable for him. If you genuinely want to make the relationship less stressful for the other person, that is consideration, not phoniness.

Furthermore, we are all four-style people. Each of us has a large repertoire of possible behaviors and interaction styles available for use in any given situation.[12] Style flex involves the employment of less frequently used aspects of our behavioral repertoire to promote better relationships, improved understanding, and increased performance. These less used aspects of behavior are really us, although they may not be our most typical behavior. The more a person flexes appropriately, the more natural his style flex will be.

"It's Just Another Form of Manipulation"

When we talk about consciously adjusting our behavior to match ways the other person likes to interact, some people get very upset. "Manipulation!" they say in an accusatory tone.

Of course, style flex can be used in an insincere and devious manner. But this is true of many things. Any method designed to improve communication can be used to manipulate people. For instance, although language can be, and often is, used for twisted purposes, that does not prevent conscientious people from using it to achieve desirable ends.

People who do take advantage of others by manipulation inevitably harm themselves. In his book on manipulation, psychologist Everett Shostrom writes: "A manipulator may be defined as a person who exploits, uses, and/or controls himself and others in certain *self*-defeating ways."[13] Psychologist Fritz Perls puts it this way:

> I call neurotic any man
> Who uses his potential to
> Manipulate the others
> Instead of growing up himself.[14]

The choice is yours. You can use style flex to manipulate others, or you can use it to create more honest and constructive relationships. We certainly don't advocate manipulating people, although we recognize that no one is totally free of the tendency to manipulate. Our personal goal is to keep manipulation at a minimum.

Not Whether You Will Flex, but How Well

The question is not whether you will flex your style. Merely to exist in this world requires some degree of style flex. All of us have learned, informally at least, some aspects of style flex. Furthermore, we practice them every day. As linguist and anthropologist Peter Farb observed,

> By the age of two or so, children already use speech . . . to talk about things they know will interest the listener, and to influence the social behavior of others. They know some of the occasions on which it is proper to shout or to whisper; they know that it is permissible to say *gimme* to certain people but that they should use *please* in other speech situations; they have some idea of differences in age and rank of listeners and the kinds of speech appropriate with a child or an adult, with a stranger or a neighbor.[15]

You flex your style unconsciously much of the time. The following chapters teach methods of *consciously* flexing your style, with sensitivity, integrity, and competence, so that mutually beneficial outcomes are more likely.

Style Flex in Action

In past years Gil Allen had been only partially successful in getting his budget approved by his boss, Joe Patterson. The meetings at which Gil presented his budget for his department had not gone well. No matter how enthusiastically Gil outlined the plans for his department, his boss seemed uninvolved. Gil's colorful visuals did not impress Patterson. Gil felt he did not get a good hearing before Patterson began eliminating major amounts related to important projects. Tension would gradually rise during the meeting, leaving everyone somewhat uncomfortable. The scenario had occured often enough so that it was highly predictable.

Last year, Gil and Roger Stokes, a colleague with whom he worked very closely, took a two-day social style course. It was then that Gil got the feedback from self-selected references that he was perceived as an Expressive. His colleague Roger was seen as an Analytical. The two discussed Joe Patterson's behavior and agreed that their boss was an Analytical.

In the upcoming fiscal year, all budgets were expected to be reduced from previous years' levels. Because of critical needs in Gil's department, he was about to present a budget that amounted to a 10 percent increase over last year. From past experience, he was not optimistic about the outcome. Yet the increase was essential if his department was to meet the company's expanded need for its services.

Gil decided to use his newly acquired style flex skills in that crucial budget meeting. He decided to flex from his own style to the Analytical style of his boss in order to increase his ability to communicate with Patterson. In preparing for the budget meeting, Gil remembered the style flex message that *how* a proposal is presented to a person of a different style can be as crucial for its acceptance as *what* the proposal contains. Gil asked Roger Stokes, his Analytical colleague, to help him figure out a better approach to the meeting. They settled on three things that Gil would do differently in order to communicate in a manner more comfortable to Patterson.

First, he would "open in parallel." Instead of using his usual way of building rapport by telling a few jokes, he would demonstrate his task orientation by keeping his informal comments brief, referring quickly to the purpose of the meeting and the importance it had to the increased responsibilities recently placed on his department. It would be a serious, low-key beginning. Second, his presentation would be concise and logical and supported by a very carefully prepared written summary with appendixes. Gil secured Roger's help in developing the presentation and in writing the support material. The third thing Gil decided to do differently was to restrain himself—talk less and listen more. He would paraphrase concerns his boss raised and then respond concisely and logically. Gil would be able to do this because he and Roger had examined the budget in detail from Patterson's point of view, in terms of both his Analytical social style and his position in the company.

When the budget and the appendixes were in final form, the two managers had a dry run, with Roger taking the role of Joe Patterson. Thus, Gil was able to flex his style in the meeting with Patterson. His budget was passed intact. Rapport was the highest it had ever been in a serious meeting between Gil and his boss.

Two days after the budget meeting, we received a letter giving a detailed description of the preparation and the meeting itself. Gil's last paragraph contained just two words: "It works!" We are obviously not claiming that by flexing your style you will inevitably achieve your goals, but we do think your ideas will get a more receptive hearing when style flex is used effectively.

When some people read this example, they say, "It took so much time and was such hard work. Was it worth it?" Gil said that for him it definitely was worth the effort because an adequate budget is so crucial to everything else he does. It is important to remember that not all style flex takes this much time. Sometimes it requires only minutes. Our guideline is to flex only when it is worth the cost in time and energy.

The next three chapters contain the information Gil and Roger drew on to manage Gil's half of the meeting more effectively.

CHAPTER 6

Excuse Me, but Your Style Is Showing

"Learning is acquired by reading books, but the much more necessary learning . . . is only to be acquired by reading men, and studying all the various editions of them." These words, written by Lord Philip Chesterfield and published in 1774,[1] are as true now as they were then.

E. L. Thorndike, the pioneering American psychologist and educator, distinguished social intelligence from two other forms of intelligence—abstract and mechanical. His definition of social intelligence specifies two components: (1) the ability to *understand* others; and (2) the ability to *act wisely* in interpersonal situations.[2] These abilities are vital to success in both personal and work life, and can be improved by the use of style recognition guidelines and by careful observation of style recognition clues.

Style Recognition Guidelines

In interpersonal relations as in most other areas of life, we suffer from information overload. Our senses are bombarded by more than our minds can process. So we need a way to concentrate on the information that best contributes to our understanding. We have to figure out what to pay attention to and what to ignore.

• *Focus only on behavior.* In social style recognition, we focus exclusively on a person's behavior.[3] To the degree that observers are objective and perceptive, they can reach agreement about the action that occurred. In social style recognition, we avoid drawing conclusions about the thoughts, attitudes, values, motives, or feelings that prompted the behavior or the meaning the event may have had for the other person.

• *Concentrate only on assertiveness and responsiveness.* When trying to recognize another person's social style, concentrate only on assertive and responsive behaviors. (Figures 2-2 and 2-4 list the behaviors characteristic of more and less assertiveness and more and less responsiveness.) Don't be distracted by other behavioral clues. First ask yourself, "Is the person's behavior more or less assertive than that of half the population?" Once you have determined that, ask yourself, "Is this person's behavior more or less emotionally controlled than that of half the population?" To make an accurate assessment of a person's social style, do not decide on a label (Driver, Amiable, Expressive, or Analytical) until after you have determined where the behavior places the person on the assertiveness and responsiveness scales. One of the most common errors in assessing social style is deciding on a style label prematurely.

• *Test your hypothesis against specific style clues.* Once you have determined a person's degree of assertiveness and responsiveness, you can determine the person's social style. Check your assessment against some of the specific clues of the style you believe the person to have. (Groups of recognition clues for each social style are found in Figure 6-1.) When you are trying to identify social style, no one clue is sufficient. Every person has elements of each style in her makeup and usually demonstrates some characteristics of several styles. It often takes time, patience, and objectivity to discern a person's dominant style from the evidence. As with most interpersonal skills, you can increase your proficiency with practice.

Figure 6-1. Groups of recognition clues for each social style.

ANALYTICAL

Less Assertive Behaviors

Slower-paced walk and gestures.
Usually talks and gestures less than the more assertive styles.
"Ask oriented," even when making statements or giving directions.
Speaks with quieter voice.
Slower, more hesitant in speech, and careful in choosing words.
May stop in midsentence, then begin a new sentence that makes more sense to the speaker, though the listener may get lost or frustrated.
Expresses ideas more tentatively and qualifies them.
Tends to lean backward when talking.
Less risk oriented; emphasizes quality— do it *right* so you don't have to do it over; careful research—focused on details, examining many opinions.
Decides more slowly.
Exerts less pressure for decisions.

Less Responsive Behaviors

Restricted body movement; gestures are fewer, smaller, and more rigid than other styles.
Little facial expression.
Little variation in voice; may tend toward monotone.
More task oriented.
More fact oriented.
Disciplined about time.
Appears to be more serious.
Appears detached from feelings.
Not apt to tell stories.
May like to work alone.

Other, Less Predictable Clues

Office decor may be tasteful, conventional, neat, and formal.
Style of dress may be more conservative, proper, and not so colorful.
May prefer solitary leisure activities; may spend more time reading; of all styles tends to spend most time doing technical reading.

Typical Characteristics

Logical, thorough, serious, systematic, prudent.

AMIABLE

Less Assertive Behaviors

Slower-paced walk and gestures.
May not talk much, especially in a group.
Soft voice; speaks less intensely.
Speaks less rapidly.
Tends to lean backward even when making a point.
Invites others to express opinions.
Tends to be quiet in meetings; may express ideas after others have spoken.
Ideas presented may be a combination of the ideas of others who have spoken; may offer a compromise or synthesis.
Expresses proposals more tentatively.
Less risk oriented; conversation may focus on guarantees.
Decides more slowly.
Exerts less pressure for decisions.

More Responsive Behaviors

People oriented; team oriented, and more apt to remember personal data about others, send birthday cards or gifts, and be concerned how people will respond or be affected by a proposed change.
Prefers one-to-one interactions or small groups to solitary activities or larger groups.
More feeling oriented; responds to feelings of others (though tries to avoid conflict and anger).
Friendly facial expression and eye contact.
Relaxed posture.
Flowing, nondramatic, nonaggressive gestures.
Moderate range of inflection.
More flexible about time.

Other, Less Predictable Clues

Office space may be informal and homey, with family pictures and so on.
Dresses informally, but in tasteful conformity.
Prefers to spend leisure time with people; emphasis in reading tends toward biographies, fiction, and inspirational literature.

Typical Characteristics

Supportive, cooperative, diplomatic, patient, loyal.

DRIVER

More Assertive Behaviors

Moves quickly.
Demonstrates task-focused energy.
Sits or stands upright or leans forward when making a point.
"Tell oriented."
May speak more rapidly.
Vocal intensity—may sound forceful without speaking loudly (some Drivers also speak loudly).
Intense eye contact when making a point.
Expresses facts and opinions more strongly.
Phrasing is direct, down to earth.
More risk oriented.
Decides more quickly.
Exerts more pressure for decisions.

Less Responsive Behaviors

Less expression in face.
More controlled body movements.
Limited variety of gestures.
Little expression in voice.

Very task oriented, pragmatic, results oriented.
Fact oriented (versus feeling and opinion oriented) but needs far fewer facts than Analyticals.
Disciplined about time.
Appears more serious.
Not apt to tell stories.
Often prefers working alone or directing others.
Interactions tend to be brief, sometimes abrupt.

Other, Less Predictable Clues

Office apt to be functional and may be spartanly decorated.
Clothing is functional, neat, action oriented, rarely splashy.
Leisure time may be spent actively; often likes competition.
Prefers brief reading material, perhaps short mystery stories or technical articles.

Typical Characteristics

Independent, candid, decisive, pragmatic, efficient.

EXPRESSIVE

More Assertive Behaviors

Fast-paced motions and gestures.
Usually brimming with energy.
Tends to speak louder than other styles.
Speaks more rapidly, with few hesitations.
Sits or stands upright or leans forward when trying to persuade.
"Tell oriented."
Expresses opinions more strongly.
More risk oriented.
Decides more quickly.
Exerts more pressure for decisions.
Initiates projects.
Dislikes routine.

More Responsive Behaviors

More large, free-flowing gestures than other styles.
Much eye contact and facial expression.
Greatest range of vocal inflection, tone, and volume.
Flowing, more dramatic use of language.
Playful and fun loving.

More apt to tell jokes and stories than other styles.
May wander from the topic.
Least disciplined about time.
People oriented—the most gregarious of the styles.
Feeling oriented—the most disclosing of the styles.
Fluctuating moods.
Has strong opinions, often based largely on intuition.

Other, Less Predictable Clues

Office may be open, colorful, bold, and disorganized; may have trophies in office or inspirational posters on wall.
Flamboyant and colorful styles of dress.
Prefers spending leisure time with people partying, competing, and so on.
Least reading oriented of the styles; may like inspirational literature.

Typical Characteristics

Outgoing, enthusiastic, persuasive, fun loving, spontaneous.

Effectiveness in style recognition involves knowing which clues are the best indicators of social style and focusing on those when making a hypothesis about another person's style. The three clusters of clues most helpful in style recognition are, in order of importance, posture and gestures, vocal clues, and verbal content. Other signals, such as office decor, clothing, and leisure activities, may help somewhat, but they are less dependable.

▪ *Train yourself to be observant.* Over a century ago, Charles Dickens wrote, "I make so bold as to believe that the faculty of closely and carefully observing . . . men is a rare one. I have not even found, within my experience, that the faculty of closely and carefully observing the faces of men, is a general one by any means."[4] Unfortunately, that condition hasn't changed much in the past 125 years. But with effort, you can train yourself to become much more attentive to the behavior of people important to your happiness and success. Style recognition depends on such accurate observation.

▪ *Don't allow first impressions to sway you.* Novices in the social style approach are apt to make snap judgments and adhere to them doggedly—even when they are wrong. Because a number of factors obscure typical behavior, first impressions of social style may often be inaccurate. Some Analyticals, for example, who have been trained in the social graces may initially act like Amiables. In time, however, such factors as their customary reserve and the strength of their task orientation become apparent. Cultural factors also affect first impressions. A Driver we know, born in the deep South, speaks and acts more slowly and graciously than is typical of Drivers. When people first meet him, they seldom think of him as a Driver. Over time, however, it becomes clear that he is a Driver who simply spends more time on social amenities than is typical of that style. Strong role requirements of a position may camouflage social style for awhile. First impressions of a police officer in our village, for example, were that he was highly assertive. When he was observed for a longer period of time, however, it became clear that he was an Amiable.

When possible, observe behavior over a significant period of time and in a variety of situations.

■ *Be aware of the confusion labels can cause.* A composite description of all the complex behaviors associated with a given social style is useful, but at the same time, the one-word label can be easily misinterpreted.[5] When the word *Driver* is used, some people conjure up visions of a tyrant with whip in hand, even though some of the world's greatest humanitarians have been Drivers. To some people, anyone who appears assertive is a Driver, even though half of the more assertive people are Expressives. When the term *Amiable* is used, some people conjure up a wishy-washy image, even though they know that many Amiables have made it to the top in fields as diverse as politics, sales, management, entertainment, athletics, education, and the military.

As outlined earlier, you can guard against allowing style labels to influence the objectivity of your observation by first assessing the person's degree of assertiveness and responsiveness over time. Then, check the style clues and select the quadrant in the social style grid that represents the person's dominant style. Finally, beware of the danger of reading negative meanings into any of the style names.

■ *Note how the person behaves under tension.* Social style usually becomes more obvious when people are under higher tension than usual. Increased tension tends to make people exaggerate their style-based behaviors. Just as a flag is hard to distinguish when there is no wind, but becomes easier to recognize when stirred by the breeze, so the winds of tension tend to make social style distinctions more obvious.

■ *Don't force classification.* At times social style classification is amazingly easy; in some instances it's nearly impossible. Although each person has characteristics of each of the styles, it is still not too difficult to determine most people's dominant style. There are some people, however, whose behaviors do not clearly put them in any particular quadrant. We estimate that for 10–20 percent of the population, it will be difficult or even impossible to determine any dominant social style.

When you are having difficulty recognizing a person's social style, be careful not to force classification. At our present state of knowledge, we know a lot but much is yet to be discovered.

■ *Treat style assessments as hypotheses.* Social style recognition skills provide working hypotheses, not absolute truths. A hypothesis needs to be tested by a search for contradictory evidence. If conflicting information is discovered, a new hypothesis is developed. When a person is classified by a typology, the assessment should always be taken with a grain of salt.

The final test of social style recognition is experimentation. After relating to a person in ways appropriate to your assessment, check the status of the relationship. If the relationship has been improved by your actions, it probably supports your reading of the other person's style. If problems have developed or deepened, a reevaluation of your assessment is necessary.

■ *Social style is but the beginning of wisdom about a person.* We have been amazed at how much the social style concept has helped us to better understand, relate to, sell to, and work with people.* When a person's social style can be accurately identified, it provides a surprising amount of information about the person. At the same time, social style pertains to only certain aspects of the person's life. Each of us is far more than our social style. Thus, identifying a person's social style is only the beginning of getting to know that person. It is one step of what can be a long and exciting journey of discovery and appreciation. As Michael Malone concluded, "The purpose should never be to lock ourselves in separate houses, but to understand better the different rooms in which we live."[6]

---

*It is one of the two most helpful applied behavioral science models we know. The other is the basic communication skills model, which teaches listening, assertion, positive reinforcement, conflict resolution, and problem-solving skills. These skills are taught in our courses, Management Communication Skills and Effective Sales Communication. The central ideas may be found in Robert Bolton's *People Skills: How to Assert Yourself, Listen to Others and Resolve Conflicts* (Englewood Cliffs, N.J.: Prentice-Hall, 1979) and in the forthcoming volume, *Management Communication Skills.*

- *Use style data constructively.* Whether used with others or with oneself, the social style model needs to be used constructively. Here are some helpful guidelines we try to follow:

  - Don't analyze a person's social style unless you want to use that information to improve your relationship.
  - Don't tell a person her social style (but if the person requests feedback from the checklists in this book, that's another matter).
  - Don't speak disparagingly about any social style, even in a joking way.

Once you have identified your own behavioral style and that of the other person in the relationship, you have information that will enable you to predict ways in which these two styles are likely to mesh and ways in which they are likely to clash. At significant points in the relationship, you can temporarily draw on some of your less frequently used behaviors to help the other person feel more comfortable with you even when talking about a stressful topic or working on a difficult project. The following chapter specifies ways to flex your behavior to get along better with people of the other social styles.

CHAPTER 7

How to Get in Sync with Others

Your objective in communication is not merely to express yourself. Your aim is to get your idea across to somebody else. Style flex provides a way of communicating on the other person's wavelength without losing your own integrity (the substance of what you say stays the same), or your naturalness (most of your behaviors will be your typical ways of relating).

The previous chapter spelled out what to look for when identifying a person's social style. Now you probably want more specific information about how to flex your style to get in sync with people whose styles are different from yours. This chapter provides specific options for flexing to each social style:

Accent behaviors you have in common.
Flex from your own style.
Increase assertiveness.
Decrease assertiveness.
Increase responsiveness.
Decrease responsiveness.
Flex to a specific social style.

This chapter deals with probabilities. Any particular Driver, for instance, may have some preferences that vary from those generally associated with Drivers. That's one reason for ongoing monitoring of how your behavior is affecting the other person.

Accenting Common Behaviors

We've already noted that style flex is, in large part, the practice of accenting the many behaviors you have in common with the other person. Discover what these are and use them appropriately. Your position on either the assertiveness or the responsiveness scale is shared with three-quarters of the population. This will help you decide which behaviors from your dominant style to continue to use in the interaction.

Notice, also, what the other person responds positively to either in you or in others. Some of his preferences will be yours, too. Accent those in your interactions with him.

Using those behaviors you have in common with another person is one of the most important guidelines for successful style flex. It lets you continue to be natural and helps you keep your own stress level low. It should constitute the major portion of most style flex interactions.

Style flex also involves temporarily adding behaviors or subtracting a few you typically use. It is helpful to remember that style flex usually involves changing only one to three types of behaviors. The many options listed in this chapter for increasing or decreasing various kinds of behavior will enable you to select the few most appropriate behaviors to use or to refrain from using in a given situation.

Flexing from Your Style

It is sometimes helpful to think of style flex not only in terms of flexing *toward* the other person's style, but also in terms of flexing *away from* your own style. Each style tends to be particularly lacking in one major area. If you are aware of this, you can adjust your behavior accordingly.

You may wish to read only the paragraphs below that contain suggestions for your style. The guidelines in this section are among the most powerful methods of style flex.

- *Drivers: listen.* Your fast-paced, goal-oriented approach often causes stress in people you work with. When you flex, make a determined effort to listen to others. Try to understand their ideas, suggestions, and requests. Equally important, listen until you understand the nature and strength of their feelings and the values and frame of reference that make their ideas worthwhile in their eyes.

In sum, concentrate on *listening* to others.

- *Expressives: restrain.* Your quick, impulsive decisions and actions, which are often based on hunches, may stress your co-workers who are less risk oriented or more fact oriented than you are. Your high energy, verbal fluency, and louder voice may intimidate them. When you flex, be sure to restrain your impulsiveness. Check the facts before making decisions. Also, when others start to speak, don't raise your voice to talk over them. Listen more. Finally, restrain your tendency to be center stage; share the limelight with others.

In sum, *restrain* your impulsiveness and desire to be talkative and center stage.

- *Amiables: stretch.* Your slower-paced, people-oriented, co-operative, low-risk approach may stress your co-workers who are faster paced and more goal oriented. When you flex, be sure to demonstrate self-determination. Set and achieve goals, and don't dodge issues—let others know where you stand. Challenge others to do their best.

In sum, *stretch* toward challenging goals and demonstrate your commitment to straight talk and results.

- *Analyticals: decide.* Your slow, systematic fact gathering, careful weighing of alternatives, and cautious decision making often stress your co-workers. When you flex, make a determined effort to decide. This means taking a stand more frequently in the discussion phase. Also, don't let your fact gathering and careful weighing of alternatives impede the progress of others. Once you have made your decision, act on it with reasonable haste.

In sum, *decide,* state your point of view, and act so that you don't hold others up.

Increasing Assertiveness

When an Analytical or an Amiable tries temporarily to flex his style toward the comfort zone of a Driver or an Expressive, he must increase his assertiveness. Here are some options to consider:

- *Posture.* Sit up straight or lean forward, but don't slouch. Keep your back straight as you lean into the conversation. Keep your feet flat on the floor. Hold your head erect; don't prop it on your hands.

- *Pace.* Speak and move faster. Decide more quickly. Drivers like to get things done in a hurry. Expressives also like to do business quickly, though they may take more time before getting down to business.

- *Intensity.* Drivers and Expressives prefer vocal intensity. Don't speak softly or slowly to these people. Let the intensity of your voice communicate that you are taking the matter seriously.

- *Gestures.* Eliminate such nonassertive gestures as shrugging the shoulders, holding your palms up, and facial expressions that may imply helplessness or avoidance of responsibility.

- *Eye contact.* Increase the frequency and intensity of your eye contact.

- *Priorities.* State your ideas and proposals positively. When possible give your recommendations to superiors rather than ask their opinion. Use direct statements rather than questions when giving directions to subordinates. Say "Please do this by noon," rather than "Can you find time to do this soon?"

- *Tenor.* Be more direct with Drivers and Expressives. State more of your disagreements, and face conflict more openly. You can object without being objectionable.

Decreasing Assertiveness

When a Driver or an Expressive tries temporarily to flex his style toward the comfort zone of an Analytical or an Amiable, he needs to decrease assertiveness. Here are options to consider:

- *Posture*. Lean back a bit and allow your body to relax more and show less energy. Don't move closer to the other person than is comfortable for him—don't invade his space.
- *Pace*. Slow down. Talk, walk, and decide less quickly. If your pace is too fast, less assertive people may feel bulldozed.
- *Intensity*. If you are an Expressive, drop the volume of your voice. If you're a Driver, eliminate some of the intensity. Try to make your point without being too loud or emphatic.
- *Gestures*. Eliminate your more forceful gestures, such as pointing your finger at the other person or banging your fist on the table.
- *Eye contact*. When making a request, have less intense and perhaps less frequent eye contact.
- *Priorities*. There are two major priorities to consider. Analyticals and Amiables tend to listen more than you do but often like to be heard themselves. Listen to what they are saying, and provide pauses to give them more of a chance to speak. Without overdoing it, invite them to speak by asking what they think about the situation and then refrain from criticizing their input. Paraphrase what they say to be sure you understand what they mean. When disagreeing, choose your words carefully and state your opinion moderately.

Another priority to consider when flexing to less assertive people is their dislike of high-risk situations. Try to find as low-risk a way of doing things as is feasible. When possible, provide guarantees and help the Amiable develop trust that you personally will stand behind your proposal. Analyticals avoid risks by their emphasis on quality and logic. If possible, join them in searching for the best solution within the constraints of cost and time. Analyze whether the various constraints are inherent to the situation or result more from your style.

■ *Tenor.* If you tend to appear cocky to others, eliminate some of that quality when dealing with less assertive people. You can often find ways to negotiate and facilitate decision making without pushing the other person into decisions. Unless you moderate your assertiveness with Amiables and Analyticals, you are apt to be seen as domineering, and this is likely to provoke resentment or resistance.

Increasing Responsiveness

When a Driver or an Analytical tries temporarily to flex his style toward the comfort zone of an Expressive or an Amiable, he needs to increase responsiveness. Here are options to consider:

■ *Gestures.* Try to loosen up a bit. Use a few more gestures, and try to make these more flowing and relaxed. Although it is hard to do, you may be able to increase your facial expressiveness in harmony with the conversation. Whether you are leaning forward or backward or sitting erect, try to have a relaxed posture while still communicating involvement.

■ *Priorities.* The more responsive styles express a people orientation. It will be important for you to find some way of touching base with these people personally. Small talk may be helpful. Amiables and Expressives often want to know how a change will affect their people. If possible, include this type of concern in your suggestions, requests, or proposals.

Amiables and Expressives are more feeling oriented. They express their own feelings and are more responsive to the feelings of others. It is important that you note and respond to their feelings. Also tune into your own feelings, and let your emotions show a bit more in your words and body language. Eliminate some of the discussion of facts and logic from your interactions with Amiables and Expressives. It's not that they are adverse to logic, but they are interested in personal opinions as well as cold facts.

■ *Tenor.* The mood preferred by Amiables and Expressives is less formal, more personal, and more fun. You can find ways of achieving goals with these people by using a lighter touch.

Decreasing Responsiveness

When an Amiable or an Expressive tries temporarily to flex his style toward the comfort zone of a Driver or an Analytical, he needs to decrease responsiveness. Here are options to consider:

■ *Gestures.* Avoid touch. Drivers and Analyticals often do not like to be slapped on the back or touched on the arm. Expressives often do well to restrain their gestures somewhat.

■ *Priorities.* These less responsive styles tend to be task oriented. Don't overdo stories, jokes, and small talk. Demonstrate your interest in helping them achieve their goals.

Drivers and Analyticals are more fact oriented, and Drivers in particular give more outward signs of their goal orientation than do most Amiables and Expressives. When relating to these people you may want to be more systematic and precise (with Analyticals) and more results oriented (with Drivers). Don't count on opinions, intuitions, and testimonies to carry much weight with these people.

■ *Tenor.* Most Drivers and Analyticals prefer a business-like approach at work. Get right to the task, stick to it on a logical and factual basis, and then leave quickly when the work is done.

Flexing to a Specific Social Style

Essentially, style flex involves adding or subtracting a few key behaviors to increase or decrease assertiveness or responsiveness. This approach can be supplemented by focusing on some of the preferences of the style you are flexing toward.* A brief summary of some preferences of each style is listed on pages 78 and 79.

*The information in this chapter has been summarized and printed in both a pocket-sized and an 8½″ × 11″ format for convenience. Either size of the Style Flex Planning Guide can be purchased from Ridge Training Resources, 5 Ledyard Avenue, Cazenovia, N.Y. 13035.

Rather than automatically following preprogrammed strategies, style flex at its best involves sensing the other's preferred ways of relating, getting in sync with some of them, monitoring the interaction, and responding to the feedback you receive from the other's behavior. Style flex needs to be undergirded with respect, fairness, and honesty. Your ability to flex your style at crucial times will contribute not only to your own effectiveness and happiness at work but also to the productivity and satisfaction of those who work with you.

Different People, Different Approaches

Chris Jackson reported to a group vice-president of a large corporation for two and one-half years. Their relationship was solid, and Chris was reviewed very favorably each year. Then her boss took early retirement. The position was filled by Dick Harlow. Chris was sorry to see her old boss leave but was open to Harlow as the new group vice-president.

Their very first meeting was far from smooth. Chris went in thoroughly prepared, as she always had been for these meetings, and began going through her list of 18 items she wanted to bring Harlow up to date on. Within ten minutes, Harlow had lit a cigarette and was smoking it in an agitated manner. After another five minutes, he was off his chair, pacing the office. Chris was uncomfortable and knew things were going poorly, but she did not know what to do other than to proceed through her detailed report. At the end of an hour-long meeting, Chris left Harlow's office with the miserable feeling that her new boss had taken an instant dislike to her.

That night Chris confided her uneasiness to her husband. As Chris described Harlow's behavior, she came to the conclusion that Harlow must be a Driver. If this were so, he probably had a different approach to meetings than his predecessor, an Analytical, had. In the past Chris was successful by being extremely thorough in her reporting. Her former boss wanted to be brought

FLEXING TO AMIABLES

Be relaxed, and moderately paced; have a comfortable posture, leaning back somewhat; speak softly, avoid harshness in voice.

Make person-to-person contact when possible. Be genuine. Don't engage in lengthy "small talk" unless it is real for you and the other person.

Invite their conversation; draw out their opinions. Listen reflectively; don't judge their ideas, counter them with logic, or manipulate.

Communicate patiently; encourage expression of any doubts, fears, or misgivings they may have. Facilitate decision making without putting excessive pressure on them.

Mutually agree on goals, perhaps initiated by you; negotiate action plans with completion dates for segments of the project; offer your cooperative support where desirable; be sure to follow through on your responsibilities; and keep in touch on theirs.

Offer personal assurance that decisions will have minimum risk. However, overstating guarantees or lack of follow-through will erode trust.

Maintain ongoing contact more than with other social styles.

FLEXING TO ANALYTICALS

Be on time.

Be moderately paced; lean back somewhat; avoid loud voice.

It is better to be more rather than less formal in clothing, speech, manners.

Get to business quickly; be prepared, systematic, factual, logical, exact—but still keep a human touch.

List the pros and cons of your proposal and of the alternatives.

Show why this approach is best and has relatively little risk. Don't exaggerate the advantages; these people are turned off by overstatement.

When possible, allow them to proceed deliberately, even slowly.

When they are too indecisive, encourage them to make a decision but refrain from making it for them.

Follow up in writing.

See that milestone dates are in the action plan; set up progress reports if in doubt about their meeting schedules.

FLEXING TO EXPRESSIVES

Be energetic and fast paced; have erect but not stiff posture and direct eye contact.

Allow time for socializing. Talk about experiences, opinions, and people. Tell about yourself, too. To a degree, adopt their entertaining, fun-loving behavior.

Expressives like arguments—to a point. Avoid becoming too dogmatic even when they are.

Discover their dreams and intuitions.

In support of your ideas, use testimonials from people they like or see as prominent.

Focus first on the "big picture." Follow up with action plans and details.

Tap their competitive spirit.

Find a way to have fun while achieving the objective.

Keep a balance between flowing with the Expressive and getting back on track.

Paraphrase agreements.

Ensure that action plans are made and followed and that necessary details are taken care of.

FLEXING TO DRIVERS

Be on time.

Be energetic and fast paced; have erect posture and direct eye contact.

Get to business quickly. Use time efficiently.

Be specific, clear, and brief. Don't overexplain, ramble, or be disorganized.

From the beginning to end, focus on results.

Select the key facts, and use them when making your case. Present them logically and quickly.

Provide a limited number of options so the Driver can make his own choice.

Provide data about the pluses and minuses of the options.

Stay on the topic; keep the pace up; and honor time limits.

If at all appropriate, ask directly for a decision.

Depart quickly but graciously.

up to date on every item and to discuss all the pros and cons, and he was slow to decide. Meetings were long and proceeded slowly. This was quite comfortable for Chris, an Amiable.

Chris, determined to improve the relationship with her new boss, reviewed the information on flexing to a Driver. She decided she couldn't do everything at once but could make some adjustments at their next meeting. She decided to (1) report on only a few selected items; (2) eliminate any detail that was not essential; and (3) quicken her pace to match her boss's better.

As usual, Chris was exactly on time for their next meeting. She began by saying, "Dick, I have 12 items I'm working on right now, but in my judgment, only three of them require your involvement. For your information I've listed the other nine items here. By concentrating on the key facts relating to the three major problems, my agenda should be over in 20–25 minutes. Do you have any additions or deletions to this agenda?"

This opening caught Harlow's attention. Chris focused on results and kept the pace rapid. The meeting was efficient, productive, and short. After the meeting Chris realized she had found a key to creating a strong working relationship with her new boss. For the two years prior to Chris's promotion, the two formed a powerful team, due in part to Chris's flexing of her style to work in ways that were most comfortable for her boss.

CHAPTER 8

Style Flex—Step by Step

By now you know quite a lot about style flex. In Chapter 5 you learned the basic concepts. Chapter 6 taught you how to recognize a person's social style. In the last chapter, you learned specific ways of flexing to each style. Assuming that you have integrated this knowledge, you could probably be fairly successful at style flex without reading further. Then why this chapter?

We found that when we used style flex we subconsciously followed a four-step problem-solving model. When we became aware of what we were doing, we began to use the process consciously. The improvement was instant. And when we began to teach managers this structure for style flex, many of them found it helpful, too. An unexpected benefit was that the person flexing could more easily pinpoint the weakest link in her efforts to flex her style. For example, we found to our surprise that managers—even those who were very successful in managing by objectives in other areas of their work—often set nonspecific or unachievable objectives for a style flex interaction.

This structured approach to style flex can help you plan and implement your part of important interactions. And it can help you evaluate how well you did in flexing your style so you can continually improve your transactions with other people by steadily increasing your style flexibility.

The Four–Step Model

Figure 8-1 summarizes the four steps of the style flex sequence.

Step 1: Diagnosing

■ *State your objective clearly and specifically*. For a number of years, we have been coaching managers in how to flex their styles. To our amazement we discovered that one of the major problems most of them had in learning to flex was that they did not know how to state their objectives. More than half the initial objectives written were too global or too subjective:

■ To regain my boss's respect.
■ To improve Monica's motivation.
■ To improve my relationship with my boss.

Common sense suggests that, with or without style flex, these broad goals could not be achieved in one session (which is all that beginners at style flex should deal with).We have learned from experience that it is often better to have a task-oriented objective than a relationship-oriented one. Many bright, logical managers do not think clearly where poor interpersonal relationships are a factor. When they use style flex to achieve worthwhile tasks, the relationships are often improved. The objective, however, should be task focused.

Setting clear, specific, and realistic objectives is possible and often essential for effective style flex. Although the following objectives could still be sharpened further, they are task oriented and specific enough to form a starting point for planning style flex:

■ To get my boss's approval of *x* advertising campaign.
■ To gain the committee's approval of the vendor certification program (for quality control).
■ To have Debbie meet the time schedule on reports every month.

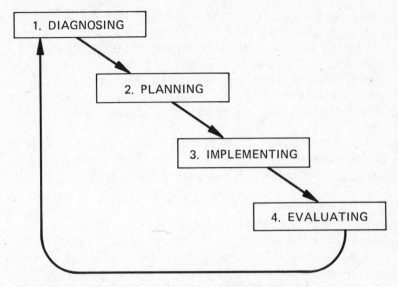

Figure 8-1. *The four-step style flex model.*

Before engaging in style flex, actually write out your objective.

■ *Do a gap analysis.* Experts on planning and problem solving often speak of doing a gap analysis. A gap analysis specifies the nature and the dimensions of the discrepancy between where a person is and where she wants to be. In style flex, a gap analysis begins with the knowledge of one's own style. Then it determines the other person's style. The differences between the customary behaviors of two persons represent the gap. With this information, you can determine the general direction your flexing should take.

There are two ways of doing a gap analysis: in your head or on paper. In your first efforts at style flex, and later in especially difficult situations, it can be helpful to sketch the situation on a "flex map."[1] A flex map is a social style grid on which you plot your dominant style and the dominant style of the person with whom you are interacting. Then you draw arrows from your location on the grid to the other's location. The lines should be parallel to the axes of the grid (see Figure 8-2).

People are tempted to take shortcuts and draw flex maps in their minds. This may be O.K. when you are experienced with the method, but when you are a novice, the graphic representation often enables you to understand the situation more clearly. Flex maps often facilitate clear thinking about difficult situations.

■ *Start where success is likely.* When you begin to use style flex consciously, select situations where you are likely to succeed. You will probably have more success at first:

- With a simple objective.
- When dealing with only one person.
- When interacting with a person with whom you have a basically good relationship.
- When flexing primarily on one scale, either the assertiveness or the responsiveness, whichever is easier for you. (It's easier for many people to move across the assertiveness scale than along the responsiveness scale.)

Step 2: Planning

Some people are turned off by the idea of planning interactions with people. However, we all plan our part of relationships much of the time. We wonder whether a coat and tie are expected at the party we are attending or whether a sport shirt will do. We wonder whether to invite the de Angelos or the Potters to dinner with the Jamisons and the Lopezes. Every now and then we talk to ourselves, rehearsing a difficult conversation we'll have during the day. When we talk about planning for style flex interactions, we are not suggesting that you try something totally new but rather that you use planning practices as you have in the past, only more skillfully.

■ *Determine what behaviors you will use.* First, determine what behaviors you have in common with the other person; these are the behaviors that you will continue. For example, an Analytical

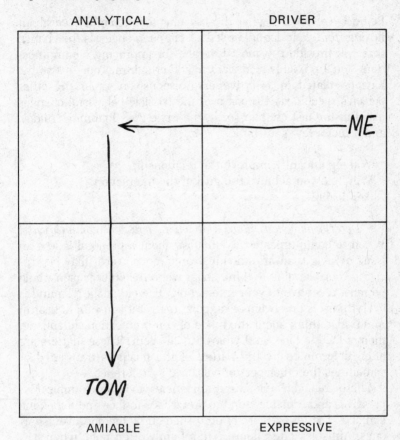

ANALYTICAL   DRIVER

ME

TOM

AMIABLE   EXPRESSIVE

*Figure 8-2. A flex map. The arrows indicate whether you have to in-
crease or decrease your assertiveness and responsiveness to
provide a more comfortable climate for the other person. More
complex flex maps may chart several people or may involve
situational factors other than people.*

and a Driver are both task oriented. When one flexes to the other,
she would continue emphasizing task accomplishment.

Next, select behaviors to add or subtract. The heart of style
flex planning is deciding how to bridge the gap between styles.

Begin by reviewing what the last chapter recommended about flexing from your dominant style. That often suggests the change that will provide the most leverage for improving communication. You'll probably also want to add or subtract one or two behaviors related to assertiveness, responsiveness, or the other person's specific style. Look over the possible behavioral changes listed in the last chapter (or in the Style Flex Planning Guide), and select a few you think:

Will significantly improve the relationship.
Will help you achieve the goal of the interaction.
Are doable.

- *Determine when, how, and where you will communicate.* When to communicate to your boss about a proposal is less an issue of style than an individual preference. Yet it may be crucial to your planning to think about when the other person would be most receptive to your interaction. The old adage "Timing is everything" is an obvious exaggeration, yet it is useful to bear in mind. Also think about the mode of communication (telephone, memo, face to face) and where it will occur. These matters are often determined by the nature of the business transacted or sometimes the other person will have a preference.

There are some style-based tendencies, too. For example, Expressives and Amiables tend to prefer face-to-face and telephone contacts. Expressives are often turned off by memos, even short ones. Amiables often appreciate a handwritten note, when it is appropriate. The action-oriented Drivers like quick transactions—the two-minute conference in the hall, a short telephone call, a brief memo. Analyticals may want to be briefed face to face or on the phone, but they often like thorough, logical follow-up in writing, or they may wish to read the proposal in advance and then discuss it with you.

Guidelines for Style Flex Planning
The following guidelines were developed from our experience with style flex.

- *Break rigid interpersonal habits.* Most of us have some behaviors that are excessively rigid. Style flex involves freeing ourselves from the domination of routines that restrict our responses and interfere with our goal attainment. It is important to moderate the interpersonal habits that have become rigid and to break the bad habits that aren't useful even in moderation.

■ *Select no more than three or four types of behaviors to alter in this interaction.* If you try too many behaviors that aren't comfortable for you, you probably won't be able to use them successfully or you may seem phony.

■ *Think about what behaviors would make the other person most comfortable in the interaction.* What bugs her most about your way of interacting? Could you eliminate that? Think of the people that get along with her best. What do they do? Can you add that?

■ *Determine which of the possible behavioral changes you can do best.* Recognize the limitations in your behavioral repertoire. Don't use behaviors that are too awkward for you.

■ *Don't overflex.* Don't try to flex too far into the other person's quadrant. Even when the other person isn't trying or hasn't been trained in the social style concept, it's rare to have to flex all the way into the other person's comfort zone. Even the most rigid person has some flexibility, and, in response to your skillful efforts at being more flexible, many people will respond with greater flexibility themselves. Effective style flex tends to pull more flexibility and adaptability from the other person. When a person overflexes (or flexes at inappropriate times), it is often seen as clumsy, patronizing, or self-serving. Overkill in style flex, as in almost anything else, is counterproductive.

When you follow these guidelines, you can flex your style and still be seen by others and by yourself as being natural, because you are continuing most of your comfortable, everyday behaviors. It is as crucial to style flex to continue most of your regular behaviors as it is to alter a few of them.

Step 3: Implementing

The social style theory is one of the rare management theories that you can implement as soon as you have the basic idea. You can begin to use style flex immediately in many situations. The other side of the coin is that mastering style flex in difficult situations may require tremendous effort and skill. It is not easy for the emotionally controlled Analytical to exude more enthusiasm when dealing with an Expressive. Similarly, it is difficult for an Expressive not to come on too strong to an Analytical. Amiables often find it tough to demonstrate their more demanding side, while Drivers usually find it hard to bring themselves to reveal their concern for people during stressful situations.

Some situations are so important that you will want to rehearse them in advance with a person who has the same social style you are flexing to. People who put weeks into the technical development of a presentation may give little or no thought to the interpersonal dynamics that can affect the outcome. Rehearsing an important interaction can help you be more comfortable as well as more effective.

You will implement better if you remember two things: the importance of empathy and the desirability of going with the flow of the other person's process. Empathy is basic to style flex. Through observation and listening, note clearly what the other person is saying and doing. Try to understand her needs in the interaction, and learn to address what's in it for her. Remember that people usually do things for their own reasons, not for yours. Knowing the other person's social style can help you listen and observe more accurately.

One of the most difficult parts of style flex is going with someone else's flow. We usually want other people to do things our way, go at our pace, use our preferred processes—that is, go with *our* flow. One reason people don't relate well when they are in their backup styles is that they tend to be nonnegotiable about the way in which they will communicate. They refuse to go with the other person's flow. Picasso exemplified this tendency when he said to Francoise Gilot, with whom he lived for a decade:

> Of course I might have said something like that. It's my nature to get angry . . . I'd like *you* to get angry, shout and

carry on, but you don't. You go silent on me, become sar-
castic, a little bitter, aloof and cold. I'd just once like to see
you spill your guts out on the table, laugh, cry—play *my*
game.[2]

Even when he wasn't in backup style, Picasso wanted people to
relate to him on his terms, using his preferred processes. That's
a nonflexible way of being with people.

By contrast, the highly flexible person makes a major effort to
tune into the other person's wavelength. Rather than fighting a
Driver's fast pace, the Amiable may accommodate it. Instead of
trying to crush the Expressive's enthusiasm, the Analytical may
work with it. Instead of trying to thwart the other person's natural processes, go with the flow of that person's preferred ways
of working and communicating.

Step 4: Evaluating

The fourth step of the social style method for creating more
productive relationships is evaluation. When you flexed your style,
did the interpersonal process improve? If it didn't, was it because of faulty diagnosis, poor planning, or inadequate implementation? If the interaction did improve, what seemed to help
most? What else might you consider doing in important conversations with this person in the future?

Two types of evaluation can improve one's style flex—*monitoring* and *postmortems*. Both types focus on your own behavior
and its consequences.

Monitoring

Monitoring is observing the effect of your behavior during the
interaction. While you are relating to other people, they are reacting to you. Through their nonverbal and verbal responses, you
can discover what you are doing that fosters better communication and what you are doing that impedes it. These observations
provide the best guide for what to do more of and what to do
less of.

A key part of monitoring is assessing the impact of your behavior on the other person's stress level. We are amazed at how rarely people are aware of rising interpersonal stress until it becomes excessive. The highly flexible person monitors the stress level of the people she is talking with.

Your sensitivity to other people's responses to what you say and do enables you to treat others as they want and deserve to be treated. This sensitivity imparts knowledge of style flex that can be learned only by experience. Monitoring is one of the most crucial skills for successful interpersonal relationships. When monitoring indicates that your behaviors are not achieving your purpose, you should immediately go back to Step 1 (diagnosing), Step 2 (planning), or Step 3 (implementing) and begin doing something differently.

Figure 8-3 sums up the activities involved in each step of the process.

Postmortems

Postmortems are evaluations that occur after the interaction. Whenever you flex your style, take time afterward to evaluate how the other person responded to your behavior. This brief evaluation can be very useful in helping you increase your style flexibility.

First, note what went right. What specifically did you do that the other person responded positively to? How specifically did she respond? Which of the behaviors that you added or subtracted seemed to have the most positive impact? Is this something you want to do more often with this person? With others of this social style?

Next, what disappointed you in your attempt to flex your style? What specifically did you do? How well did you do it? As accurately as possible, describe to yourself how the other person responded. Which of your behaviors had the least positive impact? Is this something you want to do less often with this person? With others of this social style? Or is it a matter of developing more competence and confidence with these behaviors?

People who learn from experience are able to grow and de-

PROBLEM-SOLVING PROCESS	STYLE FLEX ACTIVITIES
1. DIAGNOSING	☐ Determine your objective for this interaction. ☐ Do a gap analysis, using style recognition skills.

2. PLANNING	☐ Determine behaviors in common to continue.
	☐ Determine what you will do to flex from your own style.
	☐ Determine how to flex to the other's style:
	  ● Behaviors to add.
	  ● Behaviors to subtract.
	☐ Plan other factors:
	  ● Where?
	  ● When?
	  ● How long?
	  ● Mode of communication?

3. IMPLEMENTING	☐ Practice with someone of the other person's style. ☐ Go with the other person's flow.

4. EVALUATING	☐ Ongoing monitoring:
	  ● In general.
	  ● Of stress level.
	☐ Postmortem.

Figure 8-3. *Style flex activities that match each step of the problem-solving process. Some interactions are easier than others and do not require the degree of diagnosing, planning, implementing, and evaluating that this list may imply.*

velop. Those who do not learn from their interactions tend to perpetuate unproductive relationships. Evaluating provides a way of becoming ever more effective in mastering the other three steps.

The Style Flex Model in Action

Al Lewis was given the new responsibility of managing the management information department for the northeastern region of a large company. When we talked with him, he had defined a major problem he wanted to solve. He believed strongly in participative management and was frustrated because, try as he might, he could not get his top team of five competent managers to contribute many ideas at their weekly meetings. It was at these meetings that problems were noted, decisions made, and action plans designed. It seemed to Al that he did all the thinking, contributing, and problem solving. No one else seemed willing to jump in with either their reactions or their ideas or even their problems. Other team members confirmed that this was a problem. Al wanted training that would move his team from where they were to where he wanted them to be.

During a two-day social style workshop, Al learned style recognition skills and developed a grid showing the social style of each of his team members. His diagram is reproduced in Figure 8-4. Al decided to use the step-by-step approach to style flex.

In the diagnosis step, he did two things. First, and most difficult, he stated his objective in measurable terms. When he said he wanted to increase participation, we asked him how he could measure that increase. The measurable objective became to increase the number of contributions from all team members by an average of 60 percent. He had a group process recorder note the number of times each team member spoke during three meetings prior to his effort at style flex. He then compared this with the results achieved when he was flexing his style. He also had a subjective criterion—that the quality of the decisions would remain the same or improve.

The second part of the diagnosis involved drawing a flex map

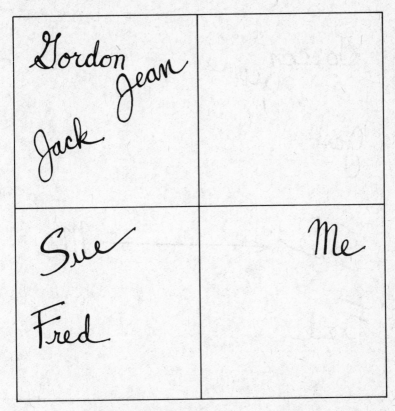

Figure 8-4. *A social style grid showing Al's assessment of each team member's style.*

(see Figure 8-5). Because he was dealing with five people rather than one, his gap analysis showed how he should flex to the group.

In the planning step, Al decided to flex only on the assertiveness dimension in his staff meetings. He chose to make four changes:

1. Stop being the first one to give his ideas (as the process recorder indicated had been his custom).

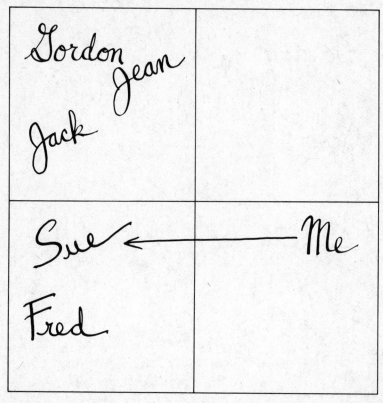

Figure 8-5. Al's flex map.

2. Decrease his participation by speaking only every third time
   he wanted to say something. (This reduced his air time
   significantly.)
3. Use listening skills to draw out the ideas of others.
4. Increase the length of meetings by up to 30 minutes (depending on the agenda) because of the slower pace of his
   less assertive team.

Part of Al's plan was also to tell his team his objective, the reason for it, and the action steps he planned to use.

Step 3, implementation, was the tough one. Although Al was only trying to modify a few behaviors, he was going against the grain of a lifetime of habit. However, he did refrain from speaking first, talked only one-third as much as previously, and used reflective listening skills. Data from the group process recorder confirmed this. Al was amazed at how stressed he got during the meeting and how tired he was at its conclusion. (This was one more confirmation of the findings that style flex can be stressful and tiring for the person doing the flexing.)

Step 4, evaluation, overlapped somewhat with implementation. As he monitored his behavior during the team session, Al thought he was flexing well, but there was little response from the team members. There were long periods of awkward silence. Nevertheless, he decided to stick to his plan.

After the session, a postmortem evaluation was led by the group process observer, with Al and the other team members participating. The report of the process observer was that Al had fulfilled his contract fairly well but that there were only a few more contributions by the other members. All involved said it was a terrible meeting. They decided, however, that it was one of those situations where conditions tend to get worse before they get better.

The team decided to continue the experiment for four more sessions. One of them said, "Al has done his part, now it's up to us to make some changes." Each member of the team committed to one or two behavioral changes in the next meeting. These were posted on a wall chart at the beginning of that meeting. By the fourth meeting, the group had hit its stride and there was no turning back. The amount of team participation increased by more than 70 percent, the quality of the decisions improved (according to Al's assessment), and the implementation of them was more effective than previously.

Five years later Al said, "It seemed traumatic at the time, but that effort at style flex had tremendous payoff. Our department grew incredibly in the past several years. Our new mode of operation helped us handle the changes and it readied my staff for the many promotions that occurred."

CHAPTER 9

Style–Based Stress Management

Stress has become a major concern for many industrial leaders—and for good reason. Stress is an increasingly serious threat to the health and productivity of Americans.

- In a nationwide study of stress at work, 83 percent of the people reported they felt they were experiencing a great deal of stress as a result of their jobs.[1]
- Stress is a major barrier to business efficiency. Some of the results of stress include:

  Reduced teamwork.
  Increased grievances.
  Needless absenteeism.
  Higher turnover rate.
  Decreased motivation.
  Poorer communication.
  Increased accidents.
  Increased antisocial acts.
  Decreased creativity.
  Increased health costs.
  Lower productivity.

- Stress is linked to managerial failure. Headhunter John Wareham says, "The key to understanding the incompetent executive is to recognize that he is rarely incompetent for technical or intellectual reasons, but that his condition is almost invariably emotional, and caused by stress."[2]
- The annual financial drain of stress on U.S. industry has been estimated at $150 billion.[3]

Alert managers are concerned about stress because it increases the cost of doing business and detracts from the quality of life of most workers. When managed well, however, stress can contribute to increased productivity and improved quality of life.

The relationship between task-oriented stress and productivity is diagrammed in Figure 9-1. When stress is excessive, pro-

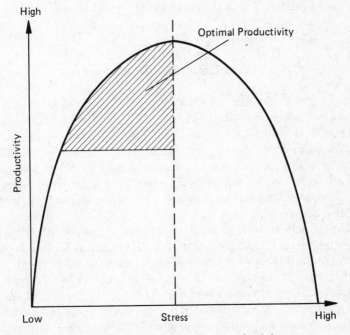

Figure 9-1. Relationship between stress and productivity.

ductivity declines. But productivity also suffers when there is an insufficient amount of constructive, task-oriented stress.[4] People in other lines of work have also learned to improve their performances by using reasonable amounts of stress constructively. The world's leading researcher on stress, Hans Selye, is well aware of the negative impact of stress on people and productivity. Yet, rather than avoiding stress, he speaks of "my intense motivation to seek a life with a purpose at the top border of my stress endurance."[5] He knows that optimal levels of constructive and well-managed stress will not only keep him productive but also add zest to his life. Selye's writings frequently refer to stress as "the spice of life."[6]

Stress is inevitable. Since it can be such an enormous factor for good or ill in our lives and in our organizations, it is important to learn to manage it well. This chapter focuses on the significant relationship between social style and stress.

Social Style and Relationship Stress

Many behavioral scientists have found it helpful to divide stress into two categories—task stress and relationship stress. Task stress is the tension generated in a person from the demands involved in doing the nonpersonal aspects of a job. Relationship stress is the tension generated in a person from the demands involved in contact with other people. One formula for success at work is to keep relationship stress low while keeping task stress constructive.

Some relationship stress is generated whenever two or more people interact, and this can provide the stimulus for positive interaction. But beyond the minimal stress that is inevitable whenever two people are in each other's presence, some additional relationship stress is usually generated. Part of that stress is good in that it contributes to our satisfaction and productivity. Much relationship stress is negative, however. Selye refers to negative stress as *distress*.[7] In this chapter (as well as in other parts of the book), we present ways to generate positive relationship stress while preventing needless relationship distress. This chapter also presents ways to handle relationship distress better when it does occur.

As we have noted, relating to people whose social styles are different from our own is apt to generate extra relationship tension. The Analytical's deliberate approach may irritate the fast-paced, impulsive Expressive. The Driver's candidness may come across as blunt and unfeeling to the Amiable. The Expressive's tendency to be talkative frustrates Analyticals, many of whom pride themselves on not wasting words. The Amiable's tendency to make fairly conservative decisions often irks the more risk-oriented Drivers. Even the body language of other styles can get under a person's skin. The emotionally expressive Winston Churchill complained to his friends about the restraint of U.S. Secretary of State John Foster Dulles, with his "great slab of a face."[8]

Sometimes the stress generated by style differences leads to job termination, even at the highest levels of large corporations. Robert P. Tyler, Jr., was dismissed as president and chief operating officer of Simmons Company. Grant G. Simmons, Jr., the chief executive officer, said the problem was incompatible management styles. Simmons says he himself is "swift to make a decision, almost to a fault," in contrast to Tyler who is "deliberate, almost to a fault."[9]

In the remainder of this chapter, we will explore ways of dealing more constructively with other people when you are under excess stress—in other words, how you can best manage yourself when you are about to go into your backup pattern. Then we'll look at the best options available when another person is in backup.

Dealing More Constructively with Your Own Backup Patterns

Fortunately, backup patterns are fairly predictable. By becoming more conscious about how you tend to react under stress, you have a greater likelihood of selecting more appropriate courses of action.

How to Prevent Yourself from Moving into Backup

It is easier to prevent backup behavior than it is to handle it effectively once it develops. People frequently operate near the critical point in terms of their stress levels. When added pressure is experienced, they have little reserve to absorb it. Here are some ways of preventing the accumulation of too much stress.

▪ *Reduce, eliminate, or divert some unnecessary pressures.* Don't agree to time schedules that are too tight. Don't give in to the impulse to overcommit. Reduce the stressors in your physical environment. Avoid or improve draining relationships. In other words, don't subject yourself to unnecessary task or relationship stress.

▪ *Identify those things you overreact to.* Usually you will find that an emotional overreaction is really a response to an un-dealt-with sore spot from your past. Ask yourself who or what event from your childhood triggered similar reactions in you. Simply understanding these connections to the past may help. Working them through with a skilled counselor can be even more beneficial.

▪ *Decrease the levels of stress that have already been generated.* Stress-reduction methods fall into two classes—those that require muscular exertion and those that require little muscular effort.

More muscular	Less muscular
Walking	Breathing relaxation
Swimming	Meditating
Jogging	Reading a book
Bike riding	Soaking in a tub
Chopping wood	Listening to music
Playing ball	Talking to a friend
Playing tennis	Playing a musical instrument
Skiing	Embroidering
Carpentry	

These activities have worked for hundreds of managers. Not all will fit your needs, nor do the lists even begin to suggest the range of possibilities. Most people tend to choose methods from one list or the other. You may find it helpful to use a few more activities from the list that is less representative of the ways you reduce stress. Most people need to spend more and better time in decreasing the levels of tension generated in modern life.

In any event, be sure to give stress a constructive outlet (including channeling it into productivity) before it gets expressed as backup behavior.

What to Do When You Find Yourself in Backup

Regardless of how effectively you handle stress, you will find yourself in your backup style some of the time. Here are some ways to minimize the difficulties your backup behavior may cause you and others.

■ *Learn to recognize when you are in your backup style.* This is difficult, because the movement from normal to backup behavior is unconscious and virtually automatic. However, if you can figure out what your primary backup style is, then you can discover the particular set of extreme, rigid, and nonnegotiable behaviors that you are prone to use under stress.

Other clues can help you discover when you are in backup style. For example, some people's breathing tends to be shallow and their shoulder muscles become tense when they are in backup. Then, too, the behaviors you pull from others can help you recognize when you are in backup. You can train yourself to know when you are in backup almost as soon as you enter it. The earlier you recognize it, the easier it is to manage this difficult part of your behavior.

■ *Catch yourself early enough to abandon your backup behavior.* We are usually able to leave our backup style if we want to. The problem is getting ourselves to choose to do the best we are capable of. The more frequently we resolve to abandon backup behavior early on, the easier it is to make that decision in the future.

There are certain things you can do to help you move out of

backup. Theologian Harry Emerson Fosdick tells how he learned
this skill:

> One of my boyhood recollections is my father's dealing with
> me when I was in a bad temper: "Where's Harry?" he would
> say, and I would answer, "Why, here he is." And he would
> say to me, "No! You are not Harry. Harry is lost. Go find
> him. I want Harry!" So, catching his meaning, I would
> wander off through the house, getting myself under control
> until returning, I could face him again, saying, "I've found
> him. Here he is."[10]

Fosdick learned to put some space between himself and others
for a short time until he got himself under control. We are not
suggesting that you repress your feelings. You can often tune in
to the full force of your feelings and still exercise behavioral self-
control.

■ If you recognize that you are in backup style and don't will
yourself out of it, *limit the interpersonal damage that you can
do.* When you are in backup, it seems as if you cannot control
your own behavior. Yet you can almost always exert some control. It is revealing to see a manager who is in backup with a
subordinate shift instantly into normal behavior when the president of the company or visiting dignitaries appear on the scene.
If that manager can control his behavior when the president walks
into the room, he can control it when only the subordinate is present. We all have far more self-control than we think.

It is not only autocratic and attacking behavior that harms relationships; avoiding and acquiescing can be just as damaging.
It can be extremely unpleasant when an Amiable in backup in-
sists on submitting to your ideas even when submission is the
last thing you want. Any extreme, rigid, and nonnegotiable behavior hurts relationships. If you don't do anything else, get
yourself out of the interpersonal situation until you are out of
your backup style. But be sure to come back when you're under
control, in order to resolve the situation.

■ *Don't make any decisions or take any crucial actions when you are in backup.* If you do, you will almost certainly regret them.

■ *Don't save your backup behavior for friends and family.* Many people learn that it is not appropriate to use backup behavior at work. So they allow their stress to build all day long and then reduce their tension by being rigid and nonnegotiable with loved ones. Their spouses and children may have been storing their tension all day long, too. When any member of the family moves into backup, it doesn't take long to get nearly everyone into their own backup styles. Many managers show less control of their backup behavior at home than anywhere else. That's a major source of the communication problem that plagues so many families.

■ *Use some stress-reduction techniques.* Such activities as those listed in the preceding section, release the stress that is the source of your backup behavior.

What to Do When Others Are in Backup

When people are in backup, they rely on a very restricted range of behaviors. At the same time, the extremism, rigidity and non-negotiability of their behaviors reduces the options of people relating to them. Here are some guidelines for making the best of a bad situation.

■ *Learn to recognize when another person is in backup.* Learn to spot each of the backup styles in action. Sometimes it is obvious that a person is in backup, but the differences between regular behavior and backup behavior are sometimes subtle. It may not be easy to tell when a normally quiet person begins to avoid or when an agreeable person shifts over to submission. Sometimes it is even difficult to know when a Driver, without raising his voice or pounding his desk, moves into quietly autocratic behavior.

Here are some ways of figuring out when a person is in backup:

1. Once you know a person's social style, you can predict the person's probable backup style (see Chapter 4).

2. For those people you spend a lot of time with, you can spot specific clues that suggest that they are in backup.
3. Note when the other person is becoming rigid and inflexible or when some of his style-based behaviors are being overused.
4. Note when you are reacting negatively to the other person. The reason may be that he is in backup.

▪ *Remember that you are probably not the real target of the other person's behavior.*[11] He is responding to inner stress, and you happened to be in the way. We are not saying that you were not the source of any of the stress, but it is unlikely that you were responsible for all of it. You'll only make matters worse by taking it personally (but not taking it personally can be tough to do).

▪ *Don't allow yourself to be controlled by the other person's counterproductive behavior.* It is foolish to let the worst behavior in the room call the plays, yet that often happens. In particular, don't allow the other person's backup behavior drive you into yours. When two or more people in the same room are directing their backup behavior at each other, it may take a long time to heal the damage.

▪ *Don't try to prevent a person from using his backup behaviors when he is under a lot of stress.* When you try to stop behaviors that are being used to relieve some of the pressure, you usually trigger even more stress in the person. Then the person is apt to become even more firmly entrenched in his extreme rigidity and unpleasant behavior.

When an Expressive is in backup, it usually does more harm than good to say, "For heaven's sake stop shouting, will you. Let's talk this over like two sane human beings." Or if it's an Analytical in silent avoidance, don't say that confiding in you will help get things off his chest. Pressuring a person to leave backup usually has the opposite of the intended effect. Obviously, however, excessive use of backup behavior over a long period of time must be confronted. If you need to discuss this with someone, do it delicately, because he may be very sensitive about it. If at all possible, wait until he is out of backup and in a low-stress period before broaching the subject.

■ *Consider whether you should try to help relieve some of the other person's pressure.* Backup behavior is at least partly a symptom of stress. If it is a subordinate who is in backup, you can monitor his workload to be sure the amount isn't too great or the deadline too tight. On the other hand, it may be that the amount of job stress is not unreasonable for the position. Harry Truman had a point when he said, "If you can't stand the heat, get out of the kitchen." Perhaps career counseling is in order.

■ *Make sure your manner of relating is constructive.* When the other person is in backup, the following are probably the best options you have:

1. Relate in ways most comfortable to the other person. (Chapters 5–8 describe how to do this.) Style flex, however, is more difficult when the other person is in backup.
2. Use conflict resolution skills.[12] Integrating style flex with conflict resolution skills is far better than using either by itself. Again, this is not easy when the other person is in backup.
3. If you don't think you can succeed with options 1 or 2, find a gracious way to stop interacting with the person. Your tactful withdrawal may help him, and it will keep you out of stressful and counterproductive interaction.

After summarizing the research on organizational stress, French and Caplan conclude that relationship stress is "the more significant organizational stress [as compared with task stress]."[13] You probably could have guessed that from your own experience.

The social style model helps managers deal with relationship stress by helping them understand that much relationship stress is caused by social style. Some of your preferred ways of relating may generate stress in the other person, and vice versa. Social style provides a basis for predicting how people are apt to act when stress gets to them.

CHAPTER 10

How People Like to Be Treated

Carl Sandburg told of the chameleon who got along very well, adjusting moment by moment to his environment, until one day he had to cross a scotch plaid. He died at the crossroads, heroically trying to blend with all the colors at once.[1] Sandburg's story suggests, in a light way, a major concern we have had about flexibility since we began teaching this model. It is not our goal to help people become human chameleons.[2]

Highly flexible people can be seen on a continuum. On one end of that continuum is a category we call "manipulators"; at the other end is a category we call "facilitators." Let's take a brief look at what these two types have in common and at some of the differences between them.

What Manipulators and Facilitators Have in Common

Manipulators and facilitators share these characteristics:

- Acute sensitivity to situations.
- A large selection of behavioral options.

- A willingness to relate in ways that are comfortable to the other person.

Sensitivity

People with high levels of sensitivity observe other people objectively and make skilled predictions of the others' probable responses. They tune into the wavelength of the people they relate to, indeed to the whole situation. They are able to assess accurately how their behaviors will be received by others. By contrast, people with low sensitivity are relatively unaware of the preferences and reactions of others. As Dan Rather said of former President Richard Nixon, "He was tone deaf on how things would appear, how they would look and sound to others."[3]

A major reason for the lack of sensitivity in some managers is their tendency to focus on the content of the discussion rather than on the *process* of the interaction. They do not read body language well and miss many of the feeling-level clues in the interaction. Nor are they aware that they should be making significant *communication decisions*—choices about whether to speak or listen, how to phrase things, and how to maintain rapport—as well as keeping track of the content of the discussion.

More responsive people, especially Amiables, tend to be more sensitive to interpersonal process than are Drivers and Analyticals. Many participants in our workshops assume that Amiables are more flexible than people of other styles. In fact, however, no social style has the edge on the other styles in terms of flexibility. A possible reason is that flexible people need not only to be sensitive but also to do something with that sensitivity. They need a sufficient repertoire of behaviors, and they have to make the decision to use it.

Extensive Behavioral Repertoire

In order to make appropriate responses to the myriad situations they confront, flexible people have developed a wide range of behavioral options. In a sense, they are like professional baseball players who learn to swing differently at fast balls, sliders, and curves. People with low flexibility, on the other hand, are like the inept ballplayer who takes the same kind of swing at any ball that is pitched. It is just as difficult for some people to assert themselves firmly as it is for others to act less aggressively. Each type of person has crucial behavioral responses that are insufficiently developed.

Choosing to Do What Is Appropriate

Sometimes people who have the sensitivity to know what is appropriate for a given situation, and who possess the ability to do it, nevertheless choose to respond in less flexible ways. When people with large behavioral repertoires choose not to exercise the appropriate option, they cancel out the effectiveness of those repertoires. The results are often detrimental to themselves, their organizations, and other people.

Differences between Manipulators and Facilitators

There is a significant difference between manipulators and facilitators. Facilitators are perceived as having high integrity.[4] Manipulators, on the other hand, are perceived over time as being low on integrity, or as being untrustworthy. When this occurs the effectiveness of manipulators suffers. Let's explore further the differences between these two types of highly flexible people.

Manipulators

The word *manipulate* means to influence by devious means, especially for one's own advantage.

> The manipulator is basically deceptive. He uses tricks, techniques and maneuvers because he cannot trust the other

person's honesty of motivation. So he puts on an act, plays roles in order to create an impression. His expressed feelings are deliberately chosen to fit the occasion. This means that he is never expressive of his true self, nor does he give another the opportunity to express his true self.[5]

Psychologist Everett Shostrom says, "For the manipulator, the understanding of human nature is for just one purpose: *control*."[6] Some people manipulate for material gain. Others enjoy the feeling of power and superiority that comes from their ability to control other people's minds and spirits. The manipulator invites you into a relationship that promises to be genuine and fulfilling, but rather than being honest in the relationship, she is bent primarily on showing off her incredible interpersonal skill.

Steersworth, in Charles Dickens's novel *David Copperfield*, exemplifies the manipulator.[7] Steersworth had the ability to charm people instantly. When he first met Peggotty, " his easy spirited good humor, his genial manner, his handsome good looks, his natural gift of adapting himself to whomsoever he pleased, and making direct, when he cared to do it, to the main point of interest in anybody's heart; bonded her to him wholly in five minutes."

Later in the evening Steersworth's amazing flexibility was even more apparent. He talked so sensitively to a shy young girl that she became assured enough to speak before the whole gathering. As the evening progressed, he laughed with some, sang with some, and talked about ships, tides, and fish when that was appropriate until David Copperfield says, "He brought us by degrees into a charmed circle, and we were all talking away without any reserve."

In the midst of this lovely portrayal, Dickens jolts us with the suggestion that Steersworth's "determination to please . . . was a brilliant game, played for the excitement of the moment . . . in the thoughtless love of superiority, in a mere wasteful, careless course of winning what was worthless to him, and the next minute throwing it away. . . ." Maybe you've had that kind of manipulator charm you and then abandon you as she moved on for more conquests.

Facilitators

In contrast to manipulators, facilitators remain genuinely themselves while understanding, respecting, and responding sensitively to other people's preferred ways of interacting. They combine strong self-esteem and depth of character with empathy and flexibility.[8] Facilitators are not conformists. When these people flex, they do not mimic other people's actions. For example, when middle-aged parents try to dress and act 20 years younger than they are, their teenage children may wish their mother and father would act their age. The human chameleon is not the model for the facilitator.

Facilitators behave appropriately with others while being true to their own values. Juan, a middle manager in a petroleum company had an early morning budget meeting with the executive vice-president of the company. The same day he had a meeting with the drilling crew in an oil patch. Clearly, the type of language appropriate in one situation would not be fitting in the other. Let's say the drilling crew used a lot of profanity and that Juan had religious convictions against swearing. Being a facilitator certainly does not require him to swear in that situation. Talking down to the men would do no good either. He could, however, select his words from the part of his vocabulary that overlapped theirs.

A term we use in this context is *integrity*. Integrity means not being phony or putting on an act. It means to ring true as a human being. Free-lance writer Arthur Gordon says: "Basically, the word means wholeness. In mathematics, an integer is a number that isn't divided into fractions. Just so, a man of integrity isn't divided against himself. He doesn't think one thing and say another. . . . He doesn't believe in one thing and do another—so he's not in conflict with his own principles."[9] In Shakespeare's words:

This above all: to thine own self be true,
And it must follow, as the night the day,
Thou canst not then be false to any man.[10]

People who are truly competent at interpersonal relationships combine personal integrity with adaptability and good communication skills. They excel at finding ways to be true to themselves without being antagonistic or abrasive to others. Unfortunately, the increasing need for flexibility in the modern world seems to be stimulating a large increase in conformity. Flexibility, when not supported by integrity, amounts to a repudiation of one's core self. As Erich Fromm puts it, "If someone violates his moral and intellectual integrity he weakens or even paralyzes his total personality."[11]

One of the tragedies of the modern era is that so many people, seeing the need to become more flexible, feel they have to choose between rigidity on the one hand and conformity or manipulation on the other. Either of these options diminishes the person and is of doubtful value to her organization or to humanity. Facilitation, however, is the option that allows a person to be true to herself while responding sensitively to other people's preferred ways of interacting.

Four Levels of Interpersonal Flexibility

As stated earlier, in some important respects, every person is:

Like all other people.
Like no other person.
More like some people than others.

Now we add a fourth to the list: In significant ways, each of us changes from one moment to the next. Corresponding to each of these four truths about people, is a level of interpersonal flexibility. Table 10-1 briefly describes each level.

Table 10-1. *Four levels of interpersonal flexibility.*

Level	Name	Focus
Level I	Basic flex(ability)	How all people want to be treated.
Level II	Style flex(ability)	How people of a given special style want to be treated.
Level III	Individual flex(ability)	How this unique individual wants to be treated.
Level IV	Existential flex(ability)	How this unique individual wants to be treated right now.

First, the flexible person treats others the way most people want to be treated. That's called *basic flex* because it's so important and is needed to undergird all other levels of interpersonal flexibility. Second, when it is appropriate, she treats a person of a certain style the way people of that style typically want to be treated. That's called *style flex*. Third, she focuses on the uniqueness of the individual. That's called *individual flex*. Finally, she responds to the changing thoughts, feelings, and priorities as they occur in the other person. That's called *existential flex*. The distinctions, though somewhat arbitrary, can help us relate more appropriately to people at work and in our personal lives.

It is our assumption that, by itself, style flex is rarely sufficient to create productive relationships. Most of this chapter deals with the crucial importance of Level I, basic flex. Levels III and IV are described briefly. Level II, style flex, has been explained in some detail in previous chapters.

Level I: Basic Flex

To gain a clearer understanding of constructive work relationships, we asked hundreds of participants in our social style workshops—managers, teachers, clergy, secretaries, salespersons, parents—to state how they liked to be treated. Three items appeared consistently on the lists. In fact, they were usually the first items mentioned:

Honestly
Fairly
With respect

Let's take a look at each of these ways of treating people that constitute what we think of as basic flex.

Honestly

Honestly is one of the first words that is called out when we ask, "How do you want to be treated?" When we ask what that means, people say they don't like being lied to, they want more feedback, and they hate being manipulated; they appreciate integrity.

Most of us think of ourselves as truthful, yet we all lie occasionally. Sometimes managers distort the truth more than is necessary or desirable—at least that's what a lot of managers tell us. Managers also tell us they want more honest feedback from their bosses and peers; they want straight talk. People need sufficient, accurate, and timely feedback from their bosses to be maximally productive. However, people tend to become distressed and defensive when they receive it. How the feedback is given can decrease the amount of distress and defensiveness. We often follow a course on social style with one on management communication skills, in which we teach how to blend straight feedback with handling predictable defensiveness.

Fairly

When we ask managers how people like to be treated, the word *fairly* is usually mentioned second. People generally assume that everyone knows what fair is. When management and labor go to the bargaining table, however, they usually disagree about what the word means. Similarly, when a subordinate talks with her boss about a raise, they may not always agree, either.

As we see it, fairness means understanding the other person's point of view and taking a win–win approach to resolving differences. By contrast, many people take a win–lose approach. Some assume that only one person can win, so they set out to defeat the other. Since no one likes to lose consistently, the win–lose approach leads to damaged relationships and lowered productivity.

Basic flex means giving due consideration to other people's needs and seeking mutually beneficial solutions.

With Respect

The other quality that is consistently mentioned when we ask how people like to be treated is *with respect*. Two components of respect crucial to basic flex are acceptance and courtesy.

■ *Acceptance*. Acceptance of another person involves behaving in ways that encourage the person to be herself. It is O.K. for her to think, manage, and live as she does as long as she doesn't interfere with your rights and productivity. Many people find it hard to distinguish between acceptance and agreement. Acceptance is the ability to demonstrate by your behavior that, even in the midst of serious disagreement, both you and the other person have a right to your own thoughts and opinions. Your disagreement need not cause you to lose respect for each other.

Acceptance also includes acceptance of the other person's social style. People have a strong tendency to devalue social styles other than their own. Long before the modern social style concept was born, the American psychologist William James divided the population into two types—the tough-minded and the tender-minded. James noted the prejudices people of one type had for people of the other:

> They have a low opinion of each other. . . . The tough think
> of the tender as sentimentalists and soft-heads. The tender
> feel the tough to be unrefined, callous, or brutal. . . . Each
> type believes the other to be inferior to itself.[12]

Such strong prejudices against other social styles are common. People may focus on the weaknesses of the other styles and overlook the strengths. They find it hard to believe that there is no best style.

An Analytical in one of our workshops was thinking of the biases that she and an Expressive had toward each other. She described their mutual nonacceptance this way:

> I act cautiously; you call it cowardly.
> You act in a way that is courageous to you
>   but foolhardy to me.
> I see myself as reserved; you see me as aloof.

■ *Courtesy.* Ideally, courtesy flows from acceptance. It is helpful to think of a range of courtesy that extends from observance of protocol, to politeness, to tact, to graciousness.

Following protocol means doing what is expected in the social environment you have chosen. It is a way of putting others at ease. Protocol involves appropriate dress and grooming. Some people couldn't care less about their appearance; they do their own thing even when co-workers think it is inappropriate. Concern for fitting appearance does not imply that clothes make the person. But it does suggest that, rightly or wrongly, indifference to such matters can trigger distrust. If you believe the expectations of the situation are undesirable, it is often wise to choose another environment.

Although the boundary between protocol and politeness is somewhat blurred, politeness is a slightly higher form of courtesy. When it is absent, the friction between people increases noticeably. We emphasize politeness here because it is missing in so many work relationships. Supervisors are often rude to hourly workers (who may have started it by being rude to the supervisors). The flexible person rises above rudeness, even when others are rude to her. (Assertion, for example, is a far better option than rudeness.) Of course, impolite behavior is not confined to hourly worker–supervisor relationships. It may be more subtle at the upper levels of the organization, but it is often present there, too. In fact, our consulting experience has shown that one of the needless problems facing many companies is impoliteness at all levels. This lowers motivation, negatively affects productivity, and chips away at employees' self-esteem.

The tactful person avoids using jargon, the special language of an in-group, except when it facilitates communication. She has a good sense of timing. Instead of blurting things out whenever they come into her head, she holds her speech until the right time. She knows when to listen and when to talk, when to laugh and when to be serious.

The spirit in which an act is done alters that behavior significantly. This distinguishes protocol and politeness from graciousness. The actions of a gracious person are characterized by kindness and warmth, tact, good taste, and generosity of spirit. Graciousness is good will expressed in little things.

Some people think they can be gracious only by concealing or compromising their convictions. What is needed is a combination of forthrightness and graciousness. An example of that unusual blend can be found in early American history. Roger Williams, the founder of Rhode Island, had a deep allegiance to values that differed greatly from those of the leaders of the Massachusetts Bay Colony, where he lived. A vigorous advocate of liberty and justice, Williams called for better treatment of the Indians. He spoke out strongly against the community's religious persecution and as a result, was banished from the colony.

It is fascinating to read the letters of this man of bold and progressive opinions. He wrote his position clearly and then would often wish his opponent well, stating his desire that the ways of God might be more fully disclosed to them both. A biographer says of this rugged pioneer, "His personal relations with men of all parties were marked by both frank controversy and friendliness. . . . Williams had learned the high act of carrying on a battle of ideas without loss of respect, esteem and affection."[13]

To sum up, basic flex means treating people with:

Honesty	*not*	Dishonesty
No lies		Lies
Straight feedback		Little or partial feedback
Straight talk		Manipulation
Integrity		Lack of integrity

Fairness	*not*	Unfairness
Understanding the other's point of view		Not understanding the other's point of view
Win–win approach		Win–lose approach

Respect	*not*	Disrespect
Acceptance		Looking down on the other person or her style
Courtesy		Lack of politeness

Basic Flex in Action

During the Civil War, Abraham Lincoln's days were long and pressured. Besides the demands of being commander in chief of the armed forces, the continuous political pressures, and the other administrative tasks requiring his attention, the president received a steady stream of visitors. Adequate screening methods were not begun until many years later, so Lincoln was subjected to nearly constant interruptions from office seekers, tourists who merely wanted to meet him, as well as people whose concerns were more serious.

One day in August 1863, the black abolitionist Frederick Douglass went to the White House to see the president. Later, in a speech, the former slave told a group of people how he was treated by Lincoln, who was working under considerable time pressure:

> I have been down there to see the President; and as you were not there, perhaps you may like to know how the

President of the United States received a black man at the White House.

I will tell you how he received me—just as you have seen one gentleman receive another; with a hand and a voice well-balanced between a kind cordiality and a respectful reserve. I tell you I felt big there! . . .

As I came in and approached him, the President began to rise, and he continued rising until he stood over me; and, reaching out his hand, he said, "Mr. Douglass, I know you; I have read about you, and Mr. Seward has told me about you"; putting me quite at ease at once.

Now, you will want to know how I was impressed by him. I will tell you that, too. He impressed me as being just what everyone of you have been in the habit of calling him—an honest man. I never met with a man who, on the first blush, impressed me more entirely with his sincerity, with his devotion to his country, and with his determination to save it at all hazards.

He told me (I think he did me more honor than I deserve) that I had made a little speech, somewhere in New York, and it had got into the papers, and among the things I had said was this: "That if I were called upon to state what I regarded as the most sad and most disheartening feature in our present political and military situation, it would not be the various disasters experienced by our armies and our navies, on flood and field, but it would be the tardy, hesitating, vacillating policy of the President of the United States; and the President said to me, "Mr. Douglass, I have been charged with being tardy, and the like"; and he went on, and partly admitted that he might seem slow; but he said, "I am charged with vacillating; but, Mr. Douglass, I do not think that charge can be sustained; I think it cannot be shown that when I have once taken a position, I have ever retreated from it."

That I regarded as the most significant point in what he said during our interview. I told him that he had been somewhat slow in proclaiming equal protection to our colored soldiers and prisoners; and he said that the country needed talking up to that point. He hesitated in regard to it, when he felt that the country was not ready for it. He knew that the colored man throughout this country was a despised man, a hated man, and that if he at first came out with such a proclamation, all the hatred which is poured on the head of the Negro race would be visited on his administration.

He said that there was preparatory work needed, and that that preparatory work had now been done. And he said "Remember this, Mr. Douglass; remember that Milliken's Bend, Port Hudson, and Fort Wagner [places where battles were fought in which black soldiers distinguished themselves for bravery] are recent events; and that these were necessary to prepare the way for this very proclamation of mine."

I thought it was reasonable, but came to the conclusion that while Abraham Lincoln will not go down to posterity as Abraham the Great, or as Abraham the Wise, or as Abraham the Eloquent, although he is all three, wise, great, and eloquent, he will go down to posterity, if the country is saved, as Honest Abraham; and going down thus, his name may be written anywhere in this wide world of ours side by side with that of Washington, without disparaging the latter.[14]

That's basic flex in action.

We have a growing appreciation for basic flex and for the difficulty of consistently expressing it in our behavior. Without a fairly high degree of Level I flexibility, style flex will do little good. Basic flex—honesty, fairness, and respect—is the foundation on which all interpersonal flexibility rests.

Level II: Style Flex

Building on basic flex as a foundation, style flex is the discipline of temporarily relating to a person in ways that are suggested by the typical preferences of that person's social style. By itself, style flex can be a shallow technique. However, when it is blended with acceptance and true graciousness it enhances relationships while making them more productive. Many of the previous chapters have dealt with style flex, so our purpose here is only to state emphatically that basic flex must accompany style flex for the latter to be effective.

Level III: Individual Flex

It is important to treat each person the way all people like to be treated, and it is sometimes also important to accommodate the style-based preferences of others, but since each person is unique, there are also times when it is important to respond to that person's individuality. Social style categories, like other generalizations, tend to ignore individuality.[15] Sometimes it is appropriate to push past the stereotypes of social style, move beyond role classification, and relate to the uniqueness of the other person.

Level IV: Existential Flex

In one of T. S. Eliot's plays, a character says, "I'm not the same person as a moment ago."[16] Keeping in touch with a person's changing moods is no easy task, yet it can be done. Existential flex means being oneself with another person as she is *right now*. Prediction helps a person attain this level, but once it is reached, prediction needs to be put aside temporarily or it will stifle spontaneous interaction.

The flexible person knows how people generally like to be treated and behaves accordingly. She is sensitive to social style differences and, drawing from her broad repertoire of behaviors, relates appropriately to other people. When the situation calls for it, she relates to the other as a unique person.

Is One Level Better Than Another?

Some people think Level IV, existential flex, is the best place to be; they want to live their lives there. To them, each succeeding level of flex seems to be better than the previous one. We don't agree, however. Level III, individual flex, and Level IV, existential flex, are often inappropriate for the modern business environment. It is fitting for many business contacts to be superficial and impersonal. What Harvey Cox writes about "urban man" is certainly true of many businesspeople:

> In most of his relationships he will be dealing with people he cannot afford to be interested in as individuals but must deal with in terms of the services they render to him and he to them. This is essential in urban life. Supermarket checkers . . . who became enmeshed in the lives of the people they were serving would be a menace. They would soon cause a total breakdown in the essential systems of which they are an integral part.[17]

Cox says that he does not mean to imply that people are to be treated as things, but they cannot always be treated as individuals.

Interpersonal flexibility is using behavior that is appropriate to the situation. Level I, basic flex—respect, fairness, and honesty—is nearly always appropriate. Level II, style flex, is appropriate some of the time. In our crowded, fast-paced world, Levels III and IV are inappropriate much of the time. On the other hand, we are human beings working with other human beings, and sometimes it will be fitting for us to relate on a personal level at work. The key is to know when to do it and to be able to relate on those levels when appropriate.

Remember, most of us can increase our flexibility significantly by going back to the basics—honesty, fairness, and respect—in our relationships. When style flex flows out of that context, it can be incredibly powerful for both persons—and for any business organization.

Conclusion

Harry Emerson Fosdick once said:

> One of the most important forks in the road of evolution came when some organisms—afterwards, clams, oysters,

crabs and lobsters—began putting their skeletons on the outside and their nerves on the inside, while others risked the great experiment of putting their skeletons within and their nerves without. So began a creature, one of whose essential characteristics was exposed sensibility.[18]

When a human being does not use her capacity for sensitivity, she spurns one of her greatest strengths. Sensitivity to other people is a virtual necessity for those whose work involves interacting with other people.

Low-flex people are behavioral monotones. Their habitual, repetitive behavior becomes irritating. They are like the old man in one of William Saroyan's stories who had but one string left on his cello. From morning until night he played just one note on that string. His patient wife finally told him that other cellists kept changing their fingers from one position to another. He laid down his bow, looked at her with a condescending smile and said, "Of course other players keep moving their fingers. They are trying to find the right place. I have found it."

However self-satisfied inflexible people may be, others tend to tire of their repetitive and often inappropriate behaviors. Low-flex people often trigger relationship stress, cause unnecessary conflict, and lower morale and productivity in the long run.

There are better and worse types of high-flex workers. Other things being equal, the facilitator has the richest personal life and makes the greatest contribution to others and to her organization. The facilitator maintains a double focus. As psychologist Clark Moustakas said, "I have lived in the deeper regions of myself and in profound resonance with others."[19] The behavior of manipulators rarely contributes to the lasting good of the organization. Further, it undercuts the well-being of fellow employees and is ultimately self-defeating. It is interesting to note that the fork in the evolutionary road that Harry Emerson Fosdick described so well, not only put the nerves on the outside of human beings, it put a backbone on the inside.

Epilogue

This model intrigues most people. They see it can help them. They want to translate the basic ideas into action. As you use social style concepts in your life, you may be helped by a warning and a paradox. Here, then, are a few thoughts we'd like to emphasize before you put the book down.

"Don't Shrink to Fit"

First, the warning. Don't shrink people to fit the social style model. This is something that requires constant vigilance. Proper use of the model helps us see ourselves and others more clearly. Overuse of the model, however, distorts perception and limits relationships. Eileen Walkenstein's caution is needed, "Don't shrink to fit."[1] People are always larger and more multifaceted than the style categories that initially help us understand them.

Some people increase their interpersonal flexibility through the social style model. However, it is not uncommon to develop a "hardening of the categories." When that happens people often become more rigid and less effective interpersonally than they were before.

You can also be too arbitrary in defining yourself in terms of your particular style. It's easy to shut off growth because you think your style doesn't excel at something. You may excuse failures and weaknesses because "Analyticals never do that sort of thing well." The simplistic use of social style often leads to a self-fulfilling prophecy: We can become as limited as the style labels we use.

So use the social style model. But be constantly vigilant about its misuse and overuse.

Easy—But Oh, So Tough

Next, the paradox. One side of the inconsistency is that social style concepts are instantly applicable. Simply knowing the ideas can be helpful. Ways to improve relationships come instantly to mind. Furthermore, without practice or training you can implement many of the things you think of. If you are like most people you will use social style concepts effortlessly in many situations.

Because the ideas are so instantly and easily applicable, people often think they have full use of the model when they are only able to use a small segment of it. That's the other side of the paradox. This model, which seems so easy to learn, cannot be fully mastered in a lifetime of effort. It's like many disciplines; the more you know, the more you see the depth and complexity of it.

In applying the social style model, use both sides of the paradox. Begin immediately to do those things you can do now to improve parts of some relationships. For those skills or situations that are more difficult for you, commit yourself to a long-term development plan. The resources listed in Appendix 4 in the back of this book may help you continue developing your expertise in applying the social style model. Some applications are difficult. Some relationships will not improve easily (and some relationships are so deeply troubled they probably won't improve at all).

No Panacea

Social style awareness is incredibly helpful to us. From it we have gained increased self-awareness and self-acceptance, and both of us do better at capitalizing on our strengths and finding ways to diminish the number of times our weaknesses trip us up. The social style model helps us understand and serve our customers better. It helps us improve our supervision and has contributed to making our organization a more positive force in employees' lives as well as a more productive business. Our life with each other, with each of our children, and with our mothers has benefitted from this model.

We're not saying that the model is a panacea. Our hopes have been dashed too often for us to believe that there are any panaceas.

Nor are we saying that we have arrived. We don't mean to leave you with that idea. In fact, just the opposite is true: We need all the help we can get. That's why the social style model means so much to us. It provides limited but significant help in those areas of life where we need it most and that are most important to us.

We're optimistic that you'll use social style concepts in your life. There is a contagion about the model. It infects and influences most people—even many who say it is simplistic or who dislike it for some other reason. Once you have the ideas, we think you'll apply them to some areas of your life even if you do it subconsciously.

If you've read this far, chances are you intend to make a conscious effort to use what you've learned. We wish you success and joy in creating satisfying and productive relationships and in further mining the ore in yourself.

APPENDIX 1

Glossary

Use the index to find more detailed discussions of these terms earlier in the book.

above the line refers to the dividing line in the social style grid that intersects the midpoint of the responsiveness axis. People "above the line" demonstrate more emotional self-control than do people "below the line." Analyticals and Drivers are located above the line.

Amiable is the social style combining higher-than-average responsiveness with a comparatively low level of assertiveness. Amiables tend to be sensitive and sympathetic to the needs of others. Of all the social styles, Amiables are most likely to use empathy and understanding in interpersonal problem solving. Typical strengths: supportive, cooperative, diplomatic, patient, loyal.

Analytical is the social style combining a high level of emotional self-control with a comparatively low level of assertiveness. Analyticals tend to take a precise, deliberate, and systematic approach to problem solving. Analyticals usually gather and evaluate much data before acting. Typical strengths: logical, thorough, serious, systematic, prudent.

assertiveness is one of the two axes of the social style grid. Assertiveness is the degree to which a person's behaviors are seen by others as being forceful or directive. The population is divided equally into the four segments, with 25 percent in each segment (see Figure 2-1).

auxiliary styles are the two social styles that a person uses less often than his dominant style but more frequently than his least developed style.

behavior refers to everything a person does that is directly observable. It includes the whole gamut of verbal and nonverbal actions.

below the line refers to the dividing line in the social style grid that intersects the midpoint of the responsiveness axis. People "below the line" demonstrate more emotional responsiveness or expressiveness than do people characterized as "above the line." The Amiable and Expressive styles are located below the line.

crucial behavioral dimensions are the two broad categories of interpersonal behavior—assertiveness and responsiveness. They are very useful in predicting how people will behave and how they prefer to be treated. A person's degree of assertiveness and responsiveness determines that person's social style.

dominant style refers to the social style most characteristic of a person. Everyone has elements of all four styles; however, one style predominates.

Driver is the social style blending a high level of emotional self-control with a high degree of assertiveness. Drivers are task-oriented people who get to the point quickly and express themselves succinctly. Typical strengths: independent, candid, decisive, pragmatic, efficient.

Expressive is the social style that integrates a high level of assertiveness with emotional expressiveness. Expressives tend to decide and act quickly. Typical strengths: outgoing, enthusiastic, persuasive, fun loving, spontaneous.

grid is the box enclosing the assertiveness and responsiveness axes (see Figure 2-5). The four social styles are contained within the quadrants.

flexibility is doing what is appropriate for the situation. There are four levels of flexibility—basic flex, style flex, individual flex, and existential flex. This concept has both similarities to and significant differences from David Merrill's and Roger Reid's concept of versatility.

least developed style is the social style in which the person is most uncomfortable and has the least competence.

left of the line refers to the dividing line in the social style grid that intersects the midpoint of the assertiveness axis. People "left of the line" demonstrate less assertiveness than do people who are "right of the line." The Amiable and Analytical styles are located left of the line.

model is a simplification of reality arrived at by overlooking individual differences to foster understanding, prediction, and action.

quadrant refers to a subsection of the grid representing one social style. The grid represents the total population of all social styles; a quadrant represents the total population of one of the social styles (see Figure 2-5).

responsiveness is one of the two axes of the social style grid. Responsiveness is the degree to which a person's behaviors are seen by others as being emotionally controlled. Responsiveness is visualized on a scale that is divided into four segments (see Figure 2-3). The population is equally divided into the four segments, with 25 percent in each.

right of the line refers to the dividing line in the social style grid that intersects the midpoint of the assertiveness axis. People "right of the line" demonstrate more assertiveness than do people "left of the line". The Driver and Expressive styles are located right of the line.

relationship stress is the tension generated from involvement with people.

social style is a pervasive and enduring pattern of interpersonal behavior. It is a model for better understanding yourself and others. The clusters of behaviors on the assertiveness and responsiveness dimensions determine a person's dominant social style.

strengths refer to the typical capabilities of each social style.

stress is the internal response of the body to any demand made upon it.

style flex is the temporary adjustment of a person's behavior to encourage others to act more productively with him. By using behavior appropriate to the other person in the particular situation, you are able to reduce the other's stress and enable him to understand your communication more clearly and perhaps be more receptive to it.

subquadrants refer to the four smaller segments into which each social style quadrant can be divided. The subquadrants permit more refined distinctions on the assertiveness and responsiveness scales (see Appendix 3).

task stress is the tension generated in a person from the demands involved in doing the nonpersonal aspects of a job.

tension see *stress*.

weaknesses are the typical liabilities of each social style.

APPENDIX 2

Social Style Model Defined

We've found that as people try to understand, accept, and apply the social style concept, they are aided greatly if they know what we mean by a model. In thinking about social style as a model for interpersonal relationships, these five ideas stand out:

- A model is a simplification of reality. It is an attempt to get to the heart of the matter by focusing on certain things and rigorously excluding others.
- A model is a generalization that is possible because it ignores individual differences.
- Reality forces us to construct interpersonal models.
- Two criteria—practical results and noncontradiction—can help us select sound models to guide our interactions.
- Because they are simplifications, even the best models have limitations.

Scientific theories are examples of the type of simplification involved in creating a model. David Landsborough Thompson notes:

In high school physics we are told about gravity and the
laws of falling bodies—thirty-two feet per second "neglect-
ing the resistance of air." The situation in real life, where
there is air and it does create friction, is much more complicated; but the fundamental law can be worked out only
by setting the complications on one side to be dealt with
later. This device runs through science. . . . The mechanics
of the heavenly bodies really could not be worked out in
terms of real objects in a real context; it was not until Gal-
ileo and Descartes taught us to think first of imaginary, ideal
objects, in empty Euclidean space, that the true laws became clear.[1]

Every worthwhile scientific discovery is a creative and drastic
simplification of reality.

The second mark of a model is a variation of the above point.
A model is a generalization because it is arrived at by leaving
out details. The process of generalizing involves noting similarities but also overlooking individual differences.[2] When we call
a certain kind of vegetable a "pea," we are generalizing. There
is a common phrase "as alike as two peas in a pod"; yet each
pea is, in some important ways, unique.[3] Generalizations are
helpful because they deal in classes and ignore the ways in which
individual objects vary.[4] Yet they can be misused precisely because they ignore individual uniqueness.

It may be necessary to create models in physical science, but
is it feasible or ethical to create models in the interpersonal
realm?[5] There is something in many people, including the authors, that reacts negatively to this. To purposely ignore individual differences in the creation and use of an interpersonal model
seems to violate the sacredness of human life. Untold evil has
been done by the generalizations people have made about people and relationships. In *Structures of Prejudice*, Carlyle Marney writes, "Prejudice is . . . wrong thinking and acting that
results from *false* generalization."[6] False generalizations about
race led to the Nazi policies of conquest and genocide. Slavery,
discrimination, and the many other tragic outcomes of prejudice

are also the result of false generalizations about interpersonal behavior.

You may wonder then how we, knowing the terrible consequences of prejudice, could write about an interpersonal model that ignores individual differences. What justification might we have for using such a model?

This brings us to the third aspect of models that helps us understand and use the social style concept. There is absolutely no way we can avoid using interpersonal generalizations. As anthropologist Edward Hall put it, "It is never possible to understand completely any other human being; and no individual will ever really understand himself—the complexity is too great."[7] Reality forces us to create interpersonal models that simplify this incredible complexity. It is impossible to live in our society without using some interpersonal models. So we must select good models, to avoid haphazard and generally ineffective ones.

The issue, then, is how to select the soundest model possible. We suggest that the model be tested against two criteria: practical results and noncontradiction.[8]

First, there is the test of results. J. J. Thompson, when Master of Trinity College, Cambridge, said, "I take the view that a theory should be a policy and not a creed, that it's most important work is to suggest things that can be tried by experiment."[9] A model is no better than its accuracy of prediction. You'll be able to test by your own experience the worth and accuracy of the social style model. Does it enable you to predict more accurately the behaviors of others? When you use it well, are you able to create more positive relationships? A key test of any model is: Does it work?

The second test of a model is noncontradiction. Does this model fit pretty well with your picture of the world? How does it square with your philosophy of life, your business sense, your ethical convictions? If one model you use is in blatant contradiction with another, further investigation is warranted. Probably one or both of the models will need to be revised or abandoned.

Finally, because they are simplifications, even the best models have their limitations. A significant model "agrees with the facts, but only more or less."[10] A model is useful "on the whole and for the most part," but not always.[11]

The philosopher Alfred North Whitehead pointed out that in order to live we are forced to simplify. The other side of the coin, according to Whitehead, is to distrust simplicity. This dual emphasis is a key to understanding and using the social style model.

APPENDIX 3

Social Style Subquadrants

There are significant differences in perceived levels of assertiveness and responsiveness within each social style. Some of these differences can be explained by further refining the social style model. It is often possible to distinguish, not only the social style quadrant, but also the subquadrant. To figure out a person's subquadrant, ask which quarters of the assertiveness and responsiveness scales are most characteristic of the person's behavior.

Charlie Jones and Sam Breen, for example, are both Drivers. Charlie is in the most assertive 25 percent of the population and the highest 25 percent in terms of emotional control. He is charted in the A-1 segment of the grid. Sam Breen is also a Driver, but he is less assertive and more emotionally expressive than Charlie. Sam is plotted in the B-2 section (see Figure A-1).

To name the subdivision of a social style, you first determine which major quadrant the person is in: Driver, Expressive, Amiable, or Analytical. That gives you the last word of the two-word description. To determine the first word, divide each quadrant into four subquadrants that correspond to the major quadrants,

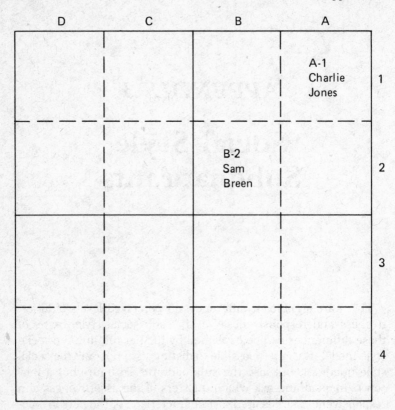

Figure A-1.   Social style grid with subquadrants.

as shown in Figure A-2. For example, Sam Breen is an Amiable Driver.

While it can sometimes be important to know which subquadrant you are in and which the other person is in, that much refinement isn't always necessary. We are repeatedly impressed by how well we can relate to others when using the broad designations of "to the left or right of the line" and "above or below the line."

D-1 Analytical ANALYTICAL	C-1 Driving ANALYTICAL	B-1 Analytical DRIVER	A-1 Driving DRIVER
D-2 Amiable ANALYTICAL	C-2 Expressive ANALYTICAL	B-2 Amiable DRIVER	A-2 Expressive DRIVER
D-3 Analytical AMIABLE	C-3 Driving AMIABLE	B-3 Analytical EXPRESSIVE	A-3 Driving EXPRESSIVE
D-4 Amiable AMIABLE	C-4 Expressive AMIABLE	B-4 Amiable EXPRESSIVE	A-4 Expressive EXPRESSIVE

Figure A-2. Names for the subquadrants of the four basic social styles.

APPENDIX 4

A List of Resources

Social Style Resources

The following resources are available for those who want to apply the social style model:

Style Flex Planning Guide—by Ridge Training Resources. Tells how to recognize and flex to each syle. Includes a style flex worksheet. Pocket size or desk size. (booklet)

StyleFlex—edited by Richard Brandon. A series of mailings designed to aid in the understanding and application of social style concepts. Assumes a basic knowledge of social styles.

Style-Based Supervision—by Robert Bolton. Goes beyond the basic concepts of style flex to consider specific guidelines for supervising people from each of the four styles. (booklet)

Job Engineering—by Robert Bolton. Style-based principles for promoting career development and for shaping the job to increase satisfaction and productivity. (booklet)

Social Styles in Team Development—by Robert Bolton and Richard Brandon. Style-based principles and practices for developing more resourceful and productive work teams. (booklet)

Personal Styles and Effective Performance—by David Merrill and Roger Reid. A presentation of the social style model and the concept of interpersonal versatility. (book)

Social Style/Selling Style—by Robert Bolton, Dorothy Grover Bolton, and Richard Brandon. Teaches the social style model as it relates to the sales process. Offers guidelines on how to open, discover needs, present, respond to objections, and close sales with customers from each of the social styles. Major segments are identical (word-for-word) to sections of *Social Style/ Management Style;* the differences between the two books are found primarily in the applications. (book)

Can Opposites Keep Attracting? Social Styles in Marriage—by Robert Bolton and Dorothy Grover Bolton. Applications of social style understandings to long-term intimate relationships. (booklet)

Social Style/Parenting Style—by Robert H. Bolton and Dorothy Grover Bolton. Tells how to develop strengths and avoid weaknesses of each parenting style. Also discusses ways to resolve most style-based conflicts between parent and parent, and between parent and child in the home. (booklet)

Social Style Profile. Computer-tabulated checklists provided by five references of the person's choice serve as the basis for feedback on the social style the person projects and on his or her interpersonal versatility. These profiles are available only at workshops and counseling sessions conducted by trainers or certified counselors.

Social Style Training. Workshops (usually lasting two days) are designed for specific types of employees: managers, supervisors, salespersons, customer relations representatives, secretaries, teachers, and others. One-day overviews and shorter presentations are also available. In the workshops an organization's trainers are instructed in conducting social style training using a social style profile.

Resources for Developing
Key Interpersonal Skills

Four clusters of skills contribute significantly to the repertoire of behaviors that increase one's resourcefulness and flexibility with people. These skill clusters are:

Listening skills
Assertion skills
Conflict resolution skills
Cooperative problem-solving skills

The following resources discuss the skill clusters:

People Skills: How to Assert Yourself, Listen to Others and Resolve Conflicts—by Robert Bolton. Explanation of how to develop each of the four primary clusters of interpersonal skills. (book)

Communication Skills Training. Courses available for specific types of employees: managers, first-line supervisors, salespersons, customer relations representatives, secretaries, teachers, and others. An organization's trainers are instructed in conducting communication skills training that can be integrated with social style awareness or can stand alone. *Family Communication Skills* courses apply the four skills to family relations.

For further information about all the resources described in this appendix, contact:

Center for Social Style Research and Application
Ridge Consultants
5 Ledyard Avenue
Cazenovia, New York 13035
(315) 655-3393

Notes and References

Preface

1. David Merrill and Roger Reid, *Personal Styles and Effective Performance: Make Your Style Work for You* (Radnor, Pa.: Chilton, 1981).
2. Carl Jung, *Psychological Types* (Princeton, N.J.: Princeton University Press, 1971).
3. Roger Stogdill and Alvin Coons, eds., *Leader Behavior: Its Description and Measurement,* Research Monograph No. 88 (Columbus: Bureau of Business Research, Ohio State University, 1957).
4. Fred Fiedler, *A Theory of Leadership Effectiveness* (New York: McGraw-Hill, 1967). See also Fred Fiedler and Martin Chemers, *Leadership and Effective Management* (Glenview, Ill: Scott, Foresman and Company, 1974); and Fred Fiedler, Martin Chemers, and Linda Mahar, *Improving Leadership Effectiveness: The Leader Match Concept,* rev. ed. (New York: John Wiley & Sons, 1977).
5. William Reddin, *Managerial Effectiveness* (New York: McGraw-Hill, 1970).
6. Albert Mehrabian, *Silent Messages* (Belmont, Calif.: Wadsworth, 1971).
7. Ernst Kretschmer, *Physique and Character: An Investigation of the Nature of Constitution and the Theory of Temperament* (New York: Cooper Square, 1970).
8. William Sheldon with S. S. Stevens, *The Varieties of Temperament: A Psychology of Constitutional Differences* (New York: Hafner, 1942).
9. Timothy Leary, *Interpersonal Diagnosis of Personality: A Func-*

tional Theory and Methodology for Personality Evaluation (New York: Ronald, 1957).

10. Everett Shostrom, *Freedom to Be: Experiencing and Expressing Your Total Being* (Englewood Cliffs, N.J.: Prentice-Hall, 1972).

11. Ralph Metzner, *Know Your Type: Maps of Identity* (Garden City, N.Y.: Anchor, 1979).

12. Robert Blake and Jane Mouton, *The New Managerial Grid* (Houston: Gulf, 1978).

13. Robert Blake and Jane Mouton, *The New Grid for Supervisory Effectiveness* (Austin, Texas: Grid Publishing, 1979).

14. Robert Blake and Jane Mouton, *The Marriage Grid* (New York: McGraw-Hill, 1971).

15. Robert Blake and Jane Mouton, *The Versatile Manager: A Grid Profile* (Homewood, Ill.: Dow Jones-Irwin, 1980).

16. Robert Blake and Jane Mouton, *Corporate Excellence through Grid Organizational Development* (Houston: Gulf, 1968).

17. Paul Hersey and Kenneth Blanchard, *Management of Organizational Behavior: Utilizing Human Resources,* 3d ed. (Englewood Cliffs, N.J.: Prentice-Hall, 1977).

18. Robert E. Lefton, V. R. Buzzotta, and Mannie Sherberg, *Dimensional Management Strategies* (St. Louis, Mo.: Psychological Associates, 1978).

19. Robert E. Lefton, V. R. Buzzotta, and Mannie Sherberg, *Improving Productivity through People Skills* (Cambridge, Mass.: Ballinger, 1980).

20. Robert E. Lefton, V. R. Buzzotta, Mannie Sherberg, and Dean Karraker, *Effective Motivation through Performance Appraisal* (New York: John Wiley & Sons, 1977).

21. Wilson Learning Corporation: *Managing Interpersonal Relationships* (Eden Prairy, Minn., 1975). This is not sold separately but is available to people who take a course there.

22. Phillip Hunsaker and Anthony Alessandra, *The Art of Managing People* (Englewood Cliffs, N.J.: Prentice-Hall, 1980).

23. Anthony Alessandra and Phillip Wexler with Jerry Dean, *Non-Manipulative Selling* (San Diego, Calif.: Courseware, 1979).

24. Michael Maccoby, *The Gamesman* (New York: Bantam, 1978).

25. Michael Maccoby, *The Leader* (New York: Simon & Schuster, 1981).

26. Jard DeVille, *Nice Guys Finish First* (New York: William Morrow, 1979).

27. Henry Golightly, *Managing with Style and Making It Work for You* (New York: AMACOM, 1977).

28. Stuart Atkins, *The Name of Your Game* (Beverly Hills, Calif.: Ellis & Stewart, 1981).

29. Isabel Myers with Peter Myers, *Gifts Differing* (Palo Alto, Calif.: Consulting Psychologists Press, 1980).

30. David Keirsey and Marilyn Bates, *Please Understand Me: An Essay on Temperament Styles* (Delmar, Calif.: Promethian Books, 1978).
31. Marie-Louise von Franz and James Hillman, *Jung's Typology* (Zurich: Spring Publications, 1975).
32. Gordon Lawrence, *People Types and Tiger Stripes: A Practical Guide to Learning Styles* (Gainesville, Fla.: Center for Applications of Psychological Type, 1979).
33. Anita Simon and Claudia Byram, *You've Got to Reach 'Em to Teach 'Em: The Teacher's Guide to Communication Styles Technology* (Dallas: TA Press, 1977).
34. Paula Becker, Larry Bledsoe, and Paul Mok, *The Strategic Woman* (Dallas: London Enterprises, 1977).
35. John Drake, *I Speak Your Language: Follow-on Self-Development Exercises* (New York: Drake-Beam & Associates, 1973).
36. Michael Malone, *Psychetypes: A New Way of Exploring Personality* (New York: Pocket Books, 1977).
37. Thomas Ritt, Jr., *Understanding Yourself and Then Others* (People Concepts, P.O. Box 2045, Ocean, N.J. 07712, 1980).
38. William Marston, *Emotions of Normal People* (Minneapolis: Persona Press, 1979).
39. *A Manual for Using the Personal Profile System* (Performax Systems International, 1979).
40. Charles Morris, *Paths of Life* (Chicago: University of Chicago Press, 1970).
41. O. Hallesby, *Temperament and the Christian Faith* (Minneapolis: Augsburg, 1962).
42. Tim LaHaye, *Transformed Temperaments* (Wheaton, Ill.: Tyndale House, 1971).
43. Tim LaHaye, *Understanding the Male Temperament* (Old Tappan, N.J.: Fleming Revell, 1977).
44. Tim LaHaye, *Spirit-Controlled Temperament* (Wheaton, Ill.: Tyndale House, 1982).
45. Beverly LaHaye, *The Spirit-Controlled Woman* (Eugene, Oreg.: Harvest House, 1982).
46. David Yates, *What the Bible Says about Your Personality* (New York: Harper & Row, 1980).
47. Cited in Eugene Randsepp, *How Creative Are You?* (New York: G. P. Putnam, 1981), p. 148.

Chapter 1: Managing Yourself and Working with Others

1. Aldous Huxley, "Tomorrow and Tomorrow and Tomorrow," *Tomorrow and Tomorrow and Tomorrow and Other Essays* (New York: Harper & Row, 1956).

2. Niccolo Machiavelli, *The Prince*. Machiavelli has unfortunately become a symbol of political unscrupulousness, and many people have dismissed his ideas without assessing their worth. It is helpful to think of his work as the first objective, scientific analysis of the methods by which political power is obtained and kept. As with any other author, the time to wrestle with the ethical implications of a given idea is after you have understood it clearly.

3. D. H. Lawrence, *Kangaroo* (New York: Heinemann, 1953), pp. 129–130.

4. This is a paraphrase of Henry Thoreau.

5. Lewis Thomas, *Late Night Thoughts on Listening to Mahler's Ninth Symphony* (New York: Viking, 1980), p. 23.

6. Martin Buber, *The Knowledge of Man* (New York: Harper & Row, 1955), pp. 67ff.

7. David Merrill, Roger Reid, and their associates developed the concept of *versatility*, which was the starting point for our thinking about *interpersonal flexibility*. We are indebted to the pioneering work these industrial psychologists did in this area. Our own point of view has evolved over time and now is considerably different from that of Merrill and Reid. For example, the term *style flex* is not used in their published work to date, and personal conversations with them suggest that this is not included in their thinking about versatility. Nor do they isolate honesty, fairness, and respect as key elements of versatility. Those interested in comparing the two concepts can read David Merrill and Roger Reid, *Personal Styles and Effective Performance* (Radnor, Pa.: Chilton Book Company, 1981).

8. Stuart Atkins, *The Name of Your Game: Four Game Plans for Success at Home and Work* (Beverly Hills, Calif.: Ellis & Steward, 1981), p. 23.

9. Cited in Richard J. Roeber, *The Organization in a Changing Environment* (Reading, Mass.: Addison-Wesley, 1973), p. 116.

10. Morgan McCall, Jr., and Michael Lombardo, "What Makes a Top Executive?" *Psychology Today*, February 1983, pp. 26–31.

11. Merrill and Reid, *Personal Styles and Effective Performance*, pp. 219ff. Merrill's concern that extremely high flexibility (he and Reid use the word *versatility*) might be a deficit has been voiced more strongly in the last year or two. An article on their model states, "On the other hand, too much of this good thing can be detrimental to effective relationships. The person with excessive versatility appears to be too changeable, too unpredictable. Others may fear he is serving himself rather than being concerned with them." Perry Pascarella, "To Motivate Others Try Versatility," *Industry Week*, May 3, 1982. Also, more research needs to be done on the relationship of social style to success. If by success we mean rising to the very

top of the organization, all styles may not do that equally well. See, for example, A. R. Colie, "Learning to Interact with Style," *Business,* January–March, 1983.
12. Michael Maccoby, *The Gamesman* (New York: Bantam, 1978), p. 124.

Chapter 2: Social Styles

1. Of the many contributions made by David Merrill to the understanding of behavioral style, one of the most important was his insistence that the social style model be based on behavior and nothing else. This distinguishes the social style model from almost all other approaches to managerial style. David Merrill and Roger Reid, *Personal Styles and Effective Performance: Make Your Style Work for You* (Radnor, Pa.: Chilton, 1981), pp. 7ff. Some theorists who developed models based on attitudes now claim their models are behavioral, although merely saying that changes nothing. At base the other models are attitude models and partly for that reason are less helpful (by our assessment) than a sound behavioral model.
2. Ira Proghoff writes, "We see the facades of personality on the surface where man meets his fellow man on a social level, and we know that this is not the fundamental ground of man's life. Something underlies it. Further back, in the hinterland of the self, something obscure but of great power is at work. How shall we understand what this something is? That is the undertaking of depth psychology. Ira Proghoff, *Depth Psychology and Modern Man* (New York: Julian, 1969), p.4.
3. Peter Drucker, *Management: Tasks, Responsibilities, Practices* (New York: Harper & Row, 1973), pp. 424–425.
4. Albert Mehrabian, *Silent Messages* (Belmont, Calif.: Wadsworth, 1971), p. 59–62.
5. Harry Stack Sullivan's "interpersonal theory of psychiatry" helped behavioral scientists see the enormous importance of interpersonal relationships in shaping behavior. See, for example, *Conceptions of Modern Psychiatry* (Washington, D.C.: William Alanson White Psychiatric Foundation, 1947), pp. 4–5, in which Sullivan stated, "Psychiatry is the study of processes that involve or go on between people. The field of psychiatry is the field of interpersonal relations under any and all circumstances in which these relationships exist." Sullivan defined interpersonal relations more broadly than we do. The Kaiser Research Foundation's approach to types concentrated on interactions between people. "To understand a person is to have knowledge of the interpersonal techniques that he employs to avoid or minimize anxiety and of the consistent pattern of rela-

tionships that he integrates as a result of these techniques." Timothy Leary, *Interpersonal Diagnosis of Personality* (New York: Ronald, 1947), p. 9.

6. Philosopher William Hocking makes the interesting observation that "we do not begin [life] as solitary beings and then acquire community: we begin as social products and acquire the arts of solitude." Quoted in John Baillie, *Our Knowledge of God* (New York: Charles Scribner's Sons, 1939), p. 208.

7. Mehrabian, *Silent Messages*, pp. 57–59.

8. About four decades ago, psychiatrist Harry Stack Sullivan used the dominant–submissive dimension and the warmth dimension to describe how people behaved with one another. Timothy Leary, Everett Shostrom, and others also used these primary dimensions of behavior in their typologies. Numerous other classifications are remarkably similar to the social style model. Robert Carson, after investigating several models, writes, "Despite minor variations and deviations, then, there is a quite impressive amount of agreement as to the structure and content of interpersonal behavior as represented in the relevant literature." *Interaction Concepts of Personality* (Chicago: Aldine, 1969), p. 106. Carson's book and Mehrabian's *Silent Messages* are the only books on Merrill's and Reid's list of recommended readings about social style in their book *Personal Styles and Effective Performance*, p. 232.

The extensive research directed by Carroll Shartle at Ohio State University in the late 1940s and early 1950s found that leadership behavior could usefully be classified into two independent dimensions called "initiating structure" and "consideration." See Roger Stogdill and Alvin Coons, eds., *Leader Behavior: Its Description and Measurement*, Research Monograph No. 88 (Columbus: Bureau of Business Research, Ohio State University, 1957). William Reddin altered the labels and the content of the behavioral dimensions to a slight degree. The dimensions he focused on were:

Task orientation (TO). The extent to which a manager directs his own and his subordinates' efforts; characterized by initiating, organizing, and directing.

Relationships orientation (RO). The extent to which a manager has personal job relationships; characterized by listening, trusting, and encouraging.

See William Reddin, *Managerial Effectiveness* (New York: McGraw-Hill, 1970), p. 24. Task orientation has similarities to the assertiveness dimension and relationship orientation has similarities to the responsiveness dimension. Blake and Mouton's model seems also similar to, if not derived from, the Ohio State model. See Robert Blake and Jane Mouton, *The New Managerial Grid* (Houston: Gulf, 1978). The model taught by R. E. Lefton, V. R. Buzzotta, and Mannie Sherberg, *Dimensional Management Strategies* (St. Louis, Mo.: Psychological Associates, 1978), bears resemblance to this source also, although the authors credit the Kaiser Foundation's work as the source of their theory. Wilson Learning Corporation's model was developed in conjunction with Merrill's work. Hunsaker, Alessandra, and DeVille's work is based strongly on Merrill's approach.

Another study that focused on a similar two dimensions was Halpin and Winer's study of air crew commanders, which found that the two dimensions of structure and consideration could account for 83 percent of the perceived differences in leader behavior. See Andrew Halpin and Ben Winer, "A Factorial Study of the Leader Behavior Descriptions," in Stogdill and Coons, eds., *Leader Behavior*.

Some, such as Merrill and Reid and Reddin, say there is a third dimension that is not part of management style but an indicator of whether that style is being used well. The third dimension has been referred to by such words as *effectiveness, appropriateness,* and *versatility.* Mehrabian, whose work appears to have impressed Merrill, found three behavioral dimensions—responsiveness, potency (assertiveness), and like–dislike. The last is suggestive of, but significantly different from, Merrill's dimension of "versatility". We'll discuss this third dimension more thoroughly in later chapters.

9. Authorities in the assertiveness training field often speak helpfully of a continuum from submissiveness through assertiveness to aggressiveness. Robert Alberti and Michael Emmons made the distinction between these types of behaviors in their influential book, *Your Perfect Right,* 2nd ed. (San Luis Obispo, Calif.: Impact, 1971), pp. 9ff.

We have found that some people in the A segment of the social style scale are highly assertive and rarely aggressive. Others who are in the A segment are viewed as very aggressive by many people. At the other end of the scale, some D's are probably submissive most of the time, while the behavior of other D's is quietly assertive. It is inaccurate to assume that all A's are aggressive and that all D's are submissive.

10. This model was designed for use with the English-speaking, nonemotionally disturbed population of the United States. The belief that all demographic categories of this population distribute approximately the same on the assertiveness and responsiveness scales needs testing. We find the social style profile is less accurate with teenagers and nonworking young adults than with adults. Numer-

ous studies have shown that, on average, women are less assertive than men are. See Vance Packard, *The Sexual Wilderness* (New York: David McKay, 1968), pp. 338–339. Does this occur because of differing definitions of assertiveness? Or is there a real difference? Our work with women supervisors and managers has indicated a fairly representative distribution, but this was not a representative sample of women in the United States. (Our extensive work with public school teachers indicated that a majority were in the less assertive half of the continuum.) Clearly, more research is needed in this area.

The model probably will work in some other cultures, but certainly not in all cultures. For example, regarding the assertiveness dimension, the differences among people in some cultures are very limited. Abraham Maslow writes, "There are people like the Arapesh who are so mild, so friendly, so unaggressive that they have to go to extremes to find a man who is even self-assertive enough to organize their ceremonies. At the other extreme, one can find people like the Chukchi and the Dobi who are so full of hatred that one wonders what keeps them from killing one another off altogether." *Motivation and Personality* (New York: Harper & Row, 1954).

11. The ancient Chinese sage Lao-tse stated more eloquently than anyone in history the power that can be characteristic of people who are not perceived as being forceful or directive. "The softest substance in the world," said Lao-tse, "goes through the hardest." (p. 216) The persistent dripping of water erodes the hardest rock. What he says of "the best rulers" applies to some highly effective managers who are perceived as being low in assertiveness: "When their task is accomplished . . . the people all remark, 'We have done it ourselves.' " (p. 114) Lin Yutang, trans. and ed., *The Wisdom of Lao-tse* (New York: Random House, 1948). Psychiatrist Fritz Perls gives an updated version of this phenomenon in his discussion of top dogs and underdogs. *Gestalt Therapy Verbatim* (New York: Bantam, 1971), pp. 19ff.

12. The following descriptions of styles are extremely brief. Our initial intention was to use lengthy descriptions of each style, amply illustrated by biographies of famous people. That research is complete, but more extensive treatment of each style would have made the book too long for our purposes.

13. Research studies by David Merrill, Roger Reid, and their associates led them to conclude that success comes to people of all social styles if they use their styles well. "When our research was completed, we concluded that we had evidence to challenge the notion that the most successful persons in business are more assertive. In ad-

dition, responsiveness or lack of it did not appear to be consistently related to success. Successful, well-regarded career persons were found along all ranges of the assertiveness and responsiveness scales—just as were less successful individuals." Merrill and Reid, *Personal Styles and Effective Performance*, p. 219.

The Merrill group defines success "either by career position or by whether others perceive the individual as being successful." To our knowledge, however, no extensive studies have been done on the distribution of styles at the vice-president level or above, or on the percentage of chief executive officers of Fortune 500 companies, for example, who are characterized by each style.

Robert Maccoby's research, which uses a different model, but one with similarities to social style, suggests that one type of manager is much more likely to reach the top levels of the high-technology companies he studied, and perhaps other companies as well. Like Merrill, Maccoby sees successful managers as having high versatility. *The Gamesman* (New York: Bantam, 1978).

There are many ways to define success—happiness, fame, accumulation of wealth, having a sound family life, making a positive contribution to the world, doing quality work, and so forth. An interesting but difficult piece of research would be to assess the typical hierarchy of dimensions of success for each style (if any exist) and then to try to determine to what degree people of each style had achieved success according to their own standards.

14. Drucker, *Management*, p. 616.

Chapter 3: Most Commonly Asked Questions about Social Style

1. William James, *Psychology, Briefer Course* (New York: Harper, 1961), p. 179. James also said that by the time one has reached the age of 30 (we would say earlier), one's basic habits and personality pattern are fixed. Reported in George Odiorne, *MBO II: A System of Managerial Leadership for the 80's* (Belmont, Calif.: Fearon Pitman, 1979), p. 166. The truth in both statements of James defines the paradox we are examining in this section.

2. Edgar Schein, *Process Consultation: Its Role in Organization Development* (Reading, Mass.: Addison-Wesley, 1969), p. 11.

3. John Geier, in the Introduction to William Marston, *Emotions of Normal People* (Minneapolis, Minn.: Persona, 1979), p. xvii.

4. Psychotherapist Paul Tournier says, "What is very rare, so much so as to constitute almost a miracle, is to find an authoritarian person giving in, or a weak person resisting." *To Resist or To Surrender?* (Richmond, Va.: John Knox, 1964), p. 37. Based on our work with "normal" people, Tournier's point is generally on target, though overstated.

5. This is true of any typology. See, for example, Carl Jung, *Psychological Types* (Princeton, N.J.: Princeton University Press, 1971), pp. 10ff and 412ff.
6. Isabel Myers Briggs notes, "Some people dislike the idea of a dominant process and prefer to think of themselves as using all four processes [styles] equally. However, Jung holds that such impartiality, where it actually exists, keeps all of the processes relatively undeveloped." *Gifts Differing* (Palo Alto, Calif.: Consulting Psychologists Press, 1980), p. 12. We think this is as true of social styles as of psychological types.

   There are some parallels to this aspect of social style. For instance, students of body language note that "every individual has a characteristic basic posture to which he returns when he has deviated from it." F. Deutsch, "Analysis of Posture Behavior," *Psychoanalytic Quarterly,* Vol. 16 (1947), pp. 195–213.
7. Sometimes the dramatic changes that are reported are not style based—the overcoming of alcoholism, for example. At other times we are told of changes that imply changes of social style—for example, changing from a "shy" person to an "outgoing" one. When people recall their personal history in this way, there are four possibilities: (1) Although it seems to them that they have changed radically, their dominant style is still the same. Shyness is still their comfort zone, but they have increased their ability to function in ways characteristic of other styles. (2) Somehow their childhood upbringing went against the grain of their real social style, if indeed style is somewhat determined by genetic inheritance. Through their life experience or through therapy, they were able to claim their own social style. (3) Because they devalued their own social style, they tried to stop using those behaviors and substitute other ways of interacting. When we've seen this, the person's behavior seems counterfeit, rather than the real thing. (4) The other option is that the person did somehow change social style.

   Some of our trainers in the social style model can usually tell when one of the first three options has occurred if they have spent sufficient time with the person. However, since we don't know most workshop participants for a long enough period of time, we can't tell whether or not to rule out the possibility that something other than a change of social style has occurred.
8. William E. Hocking, *Human Nature and Its Remaking* (New Haven, Conn.: Yale University Press, 1918), pp. 9–10.
9. A few special circumstances, such as senility, can alter a person's social style. As far as we can tell, even psychoanalysis does not change one's style. Karen Horney's remarks, though not addressed

to issues of social style, are pertinent here. "Obviously not even analysis can change constitution. It can liberate a person whose hands and feet are tied so that he may freely use his strength again, but it cannot give him new arms and legs. But it has shown that many factors that he had believed to be constitutional are no more than consequences of blockages of growth which can be resolved." Quoted in Jack Rubius, *Karen Horney: Gentle Rebel of Psychoanalysis* (New York: Dial, 1978), p. 54.

10. As the information in Note 7 suggests, the question of whether we can know from biographies whether historical characters changed their social styles is not an easy one.

11. Ernest Jones, *The Life and Work of Sigmund Freud*, edited and abridged by Lionel Trilling and Steven Marcus (New York: Basic Books, 1961), p. 12.

12. Alfred Adler, *Problems of Neurosis* (New York: Cosmopolitan Books, 1930), p. 48.

13. Jung, *Psychological Types*, p. 516.

14. Isabel Myers Briggs points out that some people use their dominant style frequently but not skillfully. "If the dominant process is . . . undeveloped, there will not be much left of the type except its weaknesses." *Gifts Differing*, p. 84. This is an important concept that deserves further exploration.

15. Within the framework of their typology, this is a treatment goal of Jungian therapists.

16. An example of what a category is like comes from the French impressionist Cezanne. He said that when he drew an apple, he did not draw an apple, he drew appleness. He did not capture the specific form of one apple, rather he sought to express the universal pattern or idea, which is not this apple or that apple, but every apple. That's what the social style model tries to do with types of people. This is a version of the Platonic approach to universals. See Eugene Freeman and David Appel. *The Wisdom and Ideas of Plato* (Greenwich, Conn.: Fawcett, 1951), p. 159.

17. Peter Farb, *Word Play: What Happens When People Talk* (New York: Bantam, 1974), p. 216.

18. Rudolf Flesch notes the power of classification: "New classifications will often completely change our attitudes and our thinking." He heralds the economy of classification as exemplified in the 20 questions game (methodology). "Twenty questions asked by a perfect player cover a range of 1,048,576 possible solutions. In other words, if you know how, you can use twenty questions to pick the one idea in a million." *The Art of Clear Thinking* (New York: Barnes & Noble Books, 1951), pp. 119–121.

19. William Hocking's "A World View" aided our thinking and phrasing of this section. William Hocking et al., *Preface to Philosophy: Textbook,* pt. 5 (New York: Macmillan, 1947).

20. S. I. Hayakawa observes: "Where we draw the line between one class of things and another depends upon the interests we have and the purposes of the classification. For example, animals are classified in one way by the meat industry, in a different way by the leather industry, in another different way by the fur industry, and in a still different way by the biologist. None of these classifications is any more final than any of the others; each of them is useful for its purpose." S. I. Hayakawa in consultation with Arthur Berger and Arthur Chandler, *Language in Thought and Action,* 4th ed. (New York: Harcourt Brace Jovanovich, 1978), p. 200.

21. Alfred Korzybski, *Science and Sanity: An Introduction to Non-Aristotelian Systems and General Semantics* (Lancaster, Pa.: Science Press, 1933).

22. Hayakawa, *Language in Thought and Action,* p. 205.

23. Confucius, quoted in Lin Yutang, trans. and ed., *The Wisdom of Lao-tse* (New York: Random House, 1948), p. 250. The ancient Hebrews were aware of this too. See Gen. 43:30–31.

24. D. H. Lawrence, *The Rainbow* (New York: Albert and Charles Boni, 1938), p. 268. Italics are ours.

25. Fyodor Dostoevsky, *The Brothers Karamazov,* trans. Constance Garnett (New York: Modern Library, 1950), p. 132.

26. David Merrill and Roger Reid, *Personal Styles and Effective Performance: Make Your Style Work For You* (Radnor, Pa.: Chilton, 1981), p. 51.

27. Joseph Luft, *Of Human Interaction* (Palo Alto, Calif.: Mayfield Publishing, 1969).

28. Robert Burns, "To a Louse."

Chapter 4: Backup Styles: Responses to Excess Stress

1. Hans Selye, *Stress without Distress* (New York: Signet, 1974) pp. 1, 5. This concept can also be found in Selye's earlier work, *The Stress of Life* (New York: McGraw-Hill, 1956).

2. We have found a slightly higher percentage of people who say they exaggerate their style-based characteristics on the assertiveness scale, than of people who think they exaggerate behavioral clusters associated with responsiveness. Research in this area might be rewarding.

3. Karen Horney noted "four principal ways in which a person tries to protect himself against basic anxiety: affection, submissiveness,

power and withdrawal." Three of these methods are strikingly similar to the concept of backup styles in the social style model. After three of the backup style labels below, we'll give Horney's descriptions that seem to match them:

Acquiescing: "If I give in I shall not be hurt."
Autocratic: "If I have power no one can hurt me."
Avoiding: "If I withdraw, nothing can hurt me."

The Neurotic Personality of Our Time (New York: W. W. Norton, 1937), pp. 96–99.

4. Everett Shostrom, who developed a model with several similarities to the social style model, says that counterproductive behaviors are those that are farther out on either of the axes. Counterproductive behavior is characterized by rigidity. *Freedom to Be: Experiencing and Expressing Your Total Being* (New York: Bantam, 1972), pp. 42ff.

5. Samuel Warner, *Self-Realization and Self-Defeat* (New York: Grove Press, 1966), p. 173.

6. Concerning another managerial style model, Robert Blake and Jane Mouton write, "How can the concept of a dominant set of assumptions be reconciled with managerial styles that shift and change? One way is through the idea of dominant and backup styles. Not only do most managers have a dominant Grid style, they also have a backup style; sometimes even a third and fourth. A manager's backup style becomes apparent when it is difficult or impossible for him to apply his dominant Grid style. In other words, a backup style is the style a manager reverts to, particularly when under pressure, tension, strain, frustration, or in situations of conflict that cannot be solved in his characteristic way." *The New Managerial Grid* (Houston: Gulf, 1978), p. 14. See also the previous edition, *The Managerial Grid* (1964), p. 13.

7. The terms were developed by Merrill, Reid, and associates.

Everett Shostrom labels the dysfunctional extensions of the styles as "pleasing" [acquiescing], "attacking" [attacking], "controlling" [autocratic] and "withdrawing" [avoiding]. *Freedom to Be,* p. 44.

Talcott Parsons, one of the most sophisticated and systematic sociologists, stated that people interact in a normal pattern of behavior until that pattern is disturbed, in which case there are tendencies to deviate from the typical pattern. "Deviance was shown to involve . . . four directional types, those of aggressiveness [attacking] and withdrawal [avoiding] . . . and compulsive performance [autocratic] and compulsive acceptance [acquiescing]. . . . It is further shown that this paradigm, independently derived, is essentially the same as that put forth by Merton." Talcott Parsons and

Robert Bales, "The Dimensions of Action-Space" in *Working Papers in the Theory of Action* (Glencoe, Ill.: The Free Press, 1953), p. 68.

8. Using yet another approach to people types with both similarities and differences to the social style model, David Yates observed, "When a person is unable to cope with life by normal behavior, he or she will shift across the chart to the opposite traits." See *What the Bible Says about Your Personality* (New York: Harper & Row, 1980), p. 73.

9. Leo Buscaglia, *Living, Loving and Learning* (New York: Holt, Rinehart, and Winston, 1982), p. 97.

Chapter 5:   Style Flex: Building Bridges, Not Boxes

1. In a paper on Jung's typology, H. Osmond, M. Siegler, and R. Smoke report that, according to his own account, Jung's purpose in constructing his typology "was to understand the differences between his own outlook and those of Freud and Adler. He attributed the failure in mutual understanding among the analysts to differences in temperament, and hoped that his typology would enable them to see that each had a different but equally valid psychology based on his own type. . . . He felt that people were so imprisoned in their own type that they could not fully understand the viewpoint of someone of another type." "Typology Revisited: A New Perspective," *Psychological Perspectives*, Vol. 8., No. 2 (1977), pp. 206–219.

2. We think the model can be equally useful for managerial self-development, and we have been surprised that learning about style-based self-development was not an equal priority for workshop participants. We have completed much of the research for a book on that subject.

3. Plato, *The Dialogues of Plato*, tr. Benjamin Jowett, in Robert Hutchins, ed., *Great Books of the Western World* (Chicago: Encylopaedia Britannica, 1952), Vol. 7, pp. 137–138.

4. William Reddin provides helpful comments on the nonhuman as well as the human factors that define a situation. See *Managerial Effectiveness* (New York: McGraw-Hill, 1970), pp. 61ff.

5. H. Richard Niebuhr makes the point that too narrow and shallow a definition of what constitutes a situation can lead to acts that are not well informed in terms of ethical considerations. He urges viewing the micro situation in which a person is about to act from the perspective of its macro setting:

Thus our responsive actions have the character of fittingness or unfittingness. We seek to make them fit into a process of interaction. The questions we raise about them are of their fittingness or unfittingness in the *total* movement [emphasis added], the whole conversation. We seek to have them fit into the whole as a sentence fits into a paragraph in a book, a note into a chord in a movement in a symphony, as the act of eating a common meal fits into the life-long companionship of a family, as the decision of a states-man fits into the ongoing movement of his nation's life with other nations. . . .

So we have come upon the great questions of the *total context* [emphasis added] in which we respond and by means of which we interpret all the specific actions upon us. What is the time span in which our responsive actions take place? Into what history do we make these actions of ours fit? For the most part it seems that responsive man has short spans of time in view. He acts in the light of brief pasts and brief futures; and yet these short periods of his one- and four- and five-year plans are surrounded by his sense of his life-time, of his social and his human history. Hence his inter-pretations of present events are always modified by the larger contexts in which they are placed. . . .

The great religions in general . . . make their impact on us by calling into question our whole conception of what is fit-ting—that is, of what really fits in—by questioning our pic-ture of the context into which we now fit our actions. . . .

[The central work of great religions is] the redefining for us of what is fitting response in a lifetime and a history sur-rounded by eternal life, as well as by the universal society of being.

The Responsible Self: An Essay in Christian Moral Philosophy (New York: Harper & Row, 1963), pp. 97, 98, 107.
   Taking Niebuhr's "total context" approach can save people from many shallow and unethical pitfalls.
6. Peter Honey, *Face to Face: Business Communication for Results* (Englewood Cliffs, N.J.: Prentice-Hall, 1976), p. xi.
7. It would have been more accurate to conclude the sentence with "and/or situation." In this book, however, we are emphasizing the interpersonal aspects of style flex.
8. Reddin has some thought-provoking ideas about effective and in-effective style flex. *Managerial Effectiveness*, pp. 51ff.
9. Most distinctions are somewhat artificial, and this is no exception.

The process used can influence the content of the outcome. Still, we find the distinction a useful one.

10. Paul Insel and Henry Lindgren, *Too Close for Comfort: The Psychology of Crowding* (Englewood Cliffs, N.J.: Prentice-Hall, 1978), p. 148.
11. Rensis Likert, *New Patterns of Management* (New York: McGraw-Hill, 1981), pp. 93–94.
12. Edgar Schein, *Process Consultation: Its Role in Organizational Development* (Reading, Mass.: Addison-Wesley, 1969), p. 32.
13. Everett Shostrom, *Man, the Manipulator: The Inner Journey from Manipulation to Actualization* (Nashville: Abingdon Press, 1967), p. 15. Italics are ours.
14. Frederick Perls, *In and Out the Garbage Pail* (Moab, Utah: Real People Press, 1969), n.p. See also Richard Niebuhr's comments in Note 4.
15. Peter Farb, *Word Play: What Happens When People Talk* (New York: Bantam, 1974), p. 280.

Chapter 6: Excuse Me, but Your Style Is Showing

1. Philip Chesterton, *Letters to His Son,* 1774.
2. Paraphrased from Edward (E. L.) Thorndike, "Intelligence and Its Use," *Harper's,* 1920, pp. 227–235. Italics are ours.
3. One of the advantages of the social style model over other approaches to managerial style is that, since it is based on behavior, the average manager with a little video training can quickly learn to identify accurately the social styles of most people. By contrast, in most managerial style models, recognition of working styles is exceedingly difficult. Carl Jung says that in his model, "while there are doubtless individuals whose type can be recognized at first glance, in actual reality [the types] are complicated and hard to make out." *Psychological Types* (Princeton, N.J.: Princeton University Press, 1971), p. 516. See also Marie Louise von Franz and James Hillman, *Lectures on Jung's Typology* (Zurich: Spring Publications, 1971), p. 50.
4. Charles Dickens, *Dombey and Son,* ed. Alan Horsman (Oxford: Oxford University Press, 1982), Appendix A: Preface to the Cheap Edition (1858).
5. To raise the issue of the names given to the styles is to open a can of worms. On the one hand we need names. Edward deBono writes, "The use of names for units is essential for communication. Names make it possible to transfer a complex situation a piece at a time." *Lateral Thinking: Creativity Step by Step* (New York: Harper & Row, 1970), p. 208. When William Sheldon was creating his typology, however, he found that "suggestive names abound in the

literature, but none seems really adequate—*they seemed to bring with them either too little or too much* [emphasis added]." William Sheldon with S. S. Stevens, *The Varieties of Temperament* (New York: Hafner, 1942), p. 18. That problem still exists. Some people have resorted to numbering the quadrants, but then there is the implication, however much it is disclaimed, that people of a particular style are really No. 1.

Because of the need to communicate succinctly and the desirability of having a standard nomenclature, we use style names developed by Merrill. At the same time, we try to stay in touch with the danger voiced so forcefully by psychologist Paul Moustakas: "The labels we attach to people . . . are just what prevent genuine knowing. For labels and classifications make it appear that we know the other, when actually we have caught the shadow and not the substance." *Individuality and Encounter: A Brief Journey into Loneliness and Sensitivity Groups* (Cambridge, Mass.: Howard A. Doyle, 1968), p. 7.

6. Michael Malone, *Psychetypes: A New Way of Exploring Personality* (New York: Pocket Books, 1977), p. 8.

Chapter 8: Style Flex—Step by Step

1. William Reddin introduced us to the useful concept of plotting the gap on a grid. *Managerial Effectiveness* (New York: McGraw-Hill, 1970), pp. 55ff.

2. Francoise Gilot and Carlot Lake, *Life with Picasso* (New York: Avon, 1981), pp. 315–316.

Chapter 9: Style-Based Stress Management

1. R. Kahn et al., *Organizational Stress: Studies in Role Conflict and Ambiguity* (New York: John Wiley, 1964).

2. John Wareham, *Secrets of a Corporate Headhunter* (New York: Atheneum, 1980). p. 83.

3. Karl Albrecht, *Stress and the Manager: Making It Work for You* (Englewood Cliffs, N.J.: Prentice-Hall, 1979), p. 133.

4. The phenomenon is called the Yerkes-Dodson Law.

5. Hans Selye, *The Stress of My Life: A Scientist's Memoirs* (New York: Von Nostrand Reinhold, 1979), p. 33.

6. Hans Selye, *The Stress of Life*, rev. ed. (New York: McGraw-Hill, 1976), p. xv.

7. Hans Selye, *Stress without Distress* (New York: Signet, 1964).

8. John Colville, *Winston Churchill and His Inner Circle* (New York: Wyndham, 1981), p. 137.

9. *Business Week,* September 5, 1977, p. 38. See also *Business Week,* January 31, 1983, p. 24, which stated that John Cardwell resigned

from the presidency of Consolidated Foods Corporation citing "differences over policy and management style." Social style and other aspects of personal chemistry also determine who gets hired. A professional recruiter quoted in the *Wall Street Journal,* September 19, 1979, said, "More than half of the time, the technically best-qualified person isn't hired."

10. Harry Emerson Fosdick, *On Being Fit to Live With* (New York: Harper & Brothers, 1946), p. 145.

11. Laura Huxley says, when other people are difficult, "stop and realize that their irritability, irrationality, lack of consideration, coolness—in other words, their disagreeable and wounding behavior is not really aimed at you.

   You may feel as though it were, but in the majority of cases it is not. You are *not* the target, You just happen to *be* there [emphasis Huxley's]." *You Are Not the Target* (North Hollywood, Calif.: Wilshire, 1963), p. 37.

12. See Robert Bolton, *People Skills: How to Assert Yourself, Listen to Others and Resolve Conflicts* (Englewood Cliffs, N.J.: Prentice-Hall, 1979), pp. 222ff. This is also covered in our forthcoming book, *Management Communication Skills.*

13. J. P. R. French and R. D. Caplan, "Organizational Stress and Individual Strain," in *The Failure of Success* ed. Albert Marrow (New York: AMACOM, 1967).

Chapter 10: How People Like to Be Treated

1. This story came to us from a speech by Gene Bartlett.

2. Some of the presentations and writing on flexibility or versatility seem to ignore the concerns raised in the 1950s by William Whyte, Jr., *The Organization Man* (New York: Simon & Schuster, 1956), and by David Riesman, Nathaniel Glazer, and Reuel Denney, *The Lonely Crowd: A Study of Changing American Character* (New Haven, Conn.: Yale University Press, 1950).

3. Dan Rather, *The Camera Never Blinks* (New York: William Morrow, 1977), p. 220.

4. We are trying to find less abstract, more behavioral ways of expressing the ideas in this chapter.

5. Maxie Dunham, Gary Herbertson, and Everett Shostrom, *The Manipulator and the Church* (Nashville: Abingdon Press, 1968), p. 19.

6. Everett Shostrom, *Man, the Manipulator: The Inner Journey from Manipulation to Actualization* (Nashville: Abingdon Press, 1967), pp. 25–26.

7. Charles Dickens, *The Personal History of David Copperfield* (New York: Grosset & Dunlap, n.d.), pp. 311–319.

8. The facilitator is true to her values, and she has a sound set of val-

ues. This hypothesis creates a double problem for us. Values are not behaviors, and we try to avoid speaking of the inner world of values in the social style model. For many people, the problem is complicated by the fact that we state that there are some universals, that some values are more worthwhile than others.

Psychologist Abraham Maslow did some pathfinding theorizing in this area, but there has been little advance in recent years. Maslow concluded that values are necessary for physical and emotional health. "The state of being without a system of values is psychopathogenic. Human beings need a philosophy of life, religion, or a value system, just as they need sunlight, calcium and love." *Toward a Psychology of Being,* 2nd ed. (New York: D. Van Nostrand, 1968), pp. 149ff. A second point that Maslow made was that many people are now experiencing a crisis of "valuelessness." "The ultimate disease of our times is valuelessness . . . this state is more crucially dangerous than ever before in history." *Religions, Values and Peak Experiences,* (Columbus: Ohio State University Press). Finally, he contrasted worthwhile values (B-values) to those values that are not constructive (D-values). Maslow writes:

These B-values, so far as I can make out at this point are—

(1) wholeness; (unity; integration; tendency to one-ness; interconnectedness; simplicity; organization; structure; dichotomy-transcendence; order);

(2) perfection; (necessity; just-right-ness; just-so-ness; inevitability; suitability; justice; completeness; "oughtness");

(3) completion; (ending; finality; justice; "it's finished"; fulfillment; *finis* and *telos;* destiny; fate);

(4) justice; (fairness; orderliness; lawfulness; "oughtness");

(5) aliveness; (process; non-deadness; spontaneity; self-regulation; full-functioning);

(6) richness; (differentiation; complexity; intricacy);

(7) simplicity; (honesty; nakedness; essentiality; abstract, essential, skeletal structure);

(8) beauty; (rightness; form; aliveness; simplicity; richness; wholeness; perfection; completion; uniqueness; honesty);

(9) goodness; (rightness; desirability; "oughtness"; justice; benevolence; honesty);

(10) uniqueness; (idiosyncrasy; individuality; non-comparability; novelty);

(11) effortlessness; (ease; lack of strain, striving or difficulty; grace; perfect, beautiful functioning);

(12) playfulness; (fun; joy; amusement; gaiety; humor; exuberance; effortlessness);

(13) truth; honesty; reality; (nakedness; simplicity; richness; "oughtness"; beauty; pure, clean and unadulterated; completeness; essentiality);

(14) self-sufficiency; (autonomy; independence; not-needing-other-than-itself-in-order-to-be-itself; self-determining; environment-transcendence; separateness; living by its own laws).

Maslow, *Toward a Psychology of Being*, p. 83.

The dual problem presented by injecting some system of B-values into the social style flexibility model may be able to be resolved. Maslow made the interesting observation that values are facts; they can be the subject of research. In time we may be able to speak behaviorally about values and to distinguish objectively which values are better than others for promoting self-actualization, constructive relationships, and so forth. Occasionally "cans of worms" should be opened. The values—social style issue needs to be faced. Only then will we know whether it needs to be resolved.

9. Arthur Gordon, "A Foolproof Formula for Success," *Reader's Digest*, 1966.

10. William Shakespeare, *Hamlet*, act 1, scene 3, lines 79–81.

11. Erich Fromm, *Psychoanalysis and Religion* (New Haven: Yale University Press, 1950), p. 74.

12. William James, *Pragmatism* (Indianapolis: Hackett, 1981), p. 11.

13. Roland Bainton, *The Travail of Religious Liberty* (Philadelphia: Westminster Press, 1951), p. 227.

14. *Proceedings of the American Anti-Slavery Society at its Third Decade, held in the City of Philadelphia, December 3–4, 1863* (New York: 1864), pp. 116–118.

15. A children's story illustrates how the relationship between two types differs significantly from the relationship between two individuals. At one point the fox says to the prince, "To me, you are still nothing more than a little boy who is just like a hundred thousand other little boys. . . . To you, I am nothing more than a fox like a hundred thousand other foxes." But, says the fox, if the relationship deepens and we establish ties, "to me you will be unique in all the world. To you, I shall be unique in all the world." Antoine de St-Exupéry, *The Little Prince* (New York: Harcourt, Brace and World, 1971), p. 80.

16. T. S. Eliot, *The Elder Statesman* (New York: Noonday Press, 1959), p. 16.

17. Harvey Cox, *The Secular City: Secularization and Urbanization in Theological Perspective* (New York: Macmillan, 1965), p. 41.
18. Harry Emerson Fosdick, *On Being a Real Person* (New York: Harper & Brothers, 1948), p. 165.
19. Clark Moustakas, *Individuality and Encounter* (Cambridge, Mass.: Howard A. Doyle Publishing Co., 1968), p. ix.

Epilogue

1. Eileen Walkenstein, *Don't Shrink to Fit: A Confrontation with Dehumanization in Psychiatry and Psychology* (New York: Grove, 1975).

Appendix 2: Social Style Model Defined

1. David Thompson, quoted in Hans Selye, *The Stress of My Life* (New York: Van Nostrand Reinhold, 1977), p. 69. Albert Einstein once said, "A theory is more impressive, the greater is the simplicity of its premises, the more different are the kinds of things it relates and the more extended its range of applicability." Quoted in G. Tyler Miller, Jr., *Energetics, Kinetics and Life* (Belmont, Calif.: Wadsworth, 1971), p. 46. For more on the value of theoretical simplicity, see Lewis Sherrill, *The Struggle of the Soul* (New York: Macmillan, 1955), p. 101.
2. Sir William Herschel, the astronomer, was able to make his scientific contributions precisely because he consciously ignored many of the differences of particular stars. He writes:

   > When I say: "Let the stars be supposed one with another to be about the size of the sun," I only mean this is the same extensive signification in which we affirm that one with another men are of such and such a particular height. This does neither exclude the Dwarf, nor the Giant. An oak tree also is of a certain size, though it admits of great variety. And . . . we shall soon allow that by mentioning the size of Man, or of the oak tree, we speak not without some real limits. . . . If we see such conformity in the whole animal and vegetable kingdom that we can, without injury to truth, affix a certain Idea to the size of the species, it appears to me highly probable, and analogous to Nature, that the same regularity will hold good with regard to the fixt stars.

   From a letter written in 1782 to the astronomer Maskelyne; quoted in C. A. Coulson, *Science and Christian Belief* (London: Fontana, 1955), pp. 76–77.
3. Some physicians have typed people for predictive purposes. People with Type A behavior are more prone to having heart attacks than

people with Type B behavior. The distinction is statistical, however. As Jere Yates writes,

> All of us have some mixture of Type A and Type B in us, but one is usually dominant. Obviously, the purer the Type A behavior, the more dangerous it could be for you, but some words of caution are necessary here. First, being a pure Type A does put you in a statistically more dangerous group, yet you as an *individual* might never have a problem with heart disease; statistics only tell us of probabilities in groups and nothing definite for any one person.

Jere Yates, *Managing Stress* (New York: AMACOM, 1979), p. 65.

4. Wendell Johnson writes, "To any . . . scientifically oriented person, *a similarity is comprised of differences that don't make any difference*. There is a saying that a difference, to be a difference, has to make a difference." *People in Quandries* (New York: Harper & Brothers, 1947), p. 38. Italics are Johnson's.

5. After struggling with this issue, Michael Maccoby wrote:

> A word about typing people: the very mention of types embarrasses those with simplistic democratic and egalitarian values who want to believe that everyone is at once different from and equal to everyone else. Although we all should recognize that we share the same human rights, consciously or unconsciously, no one can avoid the cognitive necessity of typing people. We commonly classify people stereotypically according to differences in age (young, middle-aged, old), sex (male and female), and race (black, white, etc.).

> Types based on a single trait are from a naturalistic point of view misleading and from a moral point of view dangerous. Any single trait may have a different meaning according to a total syndrome of psychological traits. For example, high IQ in a manipulator is different from the intelligence of a wise and responsible person. Typing according to single traits also lends itself to moralism, which thrives on simple dichotomies which can be labeled good and bad. Correspondingly, moralists tend to reduce complex alternatives to dichotomies or one dimensional continua which can be treated as good (high score) vs. bad (low score).

> Bureaucracies tend to type people to fit the requirements of their hierarchies; teachers type students as bright, average, or retarded; police type criminals and law abiders; psychi-

atrists type normals, neurotics, and psychotics. Factory managers typically type workers and managers into categories of hardworking, lazy, incompetent, responsible, irresponsible, etc.—all according to how well they serve the organization. In contrast, the types we developed cut across demographic classifications according to age, sex, and race, and they are based on emotional attitudes—frame of orientation shared by a large number of people.

A true social character type cannot be labeled simply as good or bad. It describes a syndrome of traits that are adaptive to the requirements of physical and psychic survival. . . .

From a social point of view, by distinguishing types according to their own strivings and values, we are trying to develop knowledge that increases compassion, respect for differences but also understanding of what we like and dislike in ourselves and others and why. . . .

But for all our efforts, no typology of character is fully satisfying as a way of understanding any particular individual. The subject matter defies boundaries. Although he described character as "man's destiny," Heraclitus also wrote, "You could not in your going find the ends of the soul though you traveled the whole way: so deep is its Law." We recognize that although our typologies may increase understanding, they must be treated dialectically, as conceptual tools. While expanding our sense of reality, they also limit our capacity to experience the uniqueness of individuals. To resolve this dialectic, however, requires more than further conceptual development. To begin to know another person in his uniqueness, to explore his soul, is a function even more of heart than head.

The Gamesman (New York: Bantam, 1978), pp. 35–37.
In the middle of that statement is a thought-provoking concept that deserves further study:

If circumstances are favorable, such adaptation allows creative development, especially in gifted members of the type. When social conditions are no longer adaptive for a type, negative traits become stronger. For example, if farmers or craftsmen are forced into industrial hierarchies, their independent attitude tends to become negativism and obstinacy.

6. Carlyle Marney, *Structures of Prejudice* (Nashville: Abingdon Press, 1961), p. 100. Italics are ours.

7. Edward Hall, *Beyond Culture* (New York: Doubleday, 1977), p. 69.

8. These two criteria are frequently used by philosophers. See Edgar Brightman, *A Philosophy of Religion* (Englewood Cliffs, N.J.: Prentice-Hall, 1940), pp. 122ff. Brightman uses the term *coherence* rather than *noncontradiction*. The latter is less accurate but helped us keep the discussion brief.

9. J. J. Thompson, quoted in Coulson, *Science and Christian Belief*, p. 85.

10. Thomas Kuhn, *The Structure of Scientific Revolutions* (Chicago: University of Chicago Press, 1962), p. 147. Kuhn's discussion of paradigms is not easy reading, but it provides a sound orientation to the nature, benefits, and limitations of models.

11. Albert Einstein, in *Sidelights on Relativity,* said, "As far as the laws of mathematics refer to reality they are not certain. And as far as they are certain they do not refer to reality." Quoted in Sanford Berman, *Understanding and Being Understood* (San Diego, Calif.: International Communication Institute, 1969), p. 42.

Index